Frontispiece *from a plate by the Victorian photographer Frank Meadow Sutcliffe. The girls second and third from the left are wearing Cottage Shawls, while the girl on the extreme left is crocheting a similar fabric.* (Reproduced by permission of the Sutcliffe Gallery, Whitby)

Crochet Lace

An Illustrated Guide to
Making Crochet Lace Fabrics

Mary Konior

BLANDFORD

Acknowledgements

With grateful thanks:
to Teresa Withycombe, my daughter, for her
valuable help in making some of the shawls,
to babies Mark Withycombe and Benjamin
Davies, whose advent made our task such a
pleasure, and to Gertrude Kuehl of the
Knitting and Crochet Guild, for her generous
answers to my queries.

A BLANDFORD BOOK

First published in the UK 1991
by Blandford
(a Cassell imprint)
Villiers House
41/47 Strand
LONDON
WC2N 5JE

Copyright © Mary Konior 1991

Distributed in the United States
by Sterling Publishing Co., Inc.
387 Park Avenue South, New York, NY 10016-8810

Distributed in Australia
by Capricorn Link (Australia) Pty Ltd
P.O. Box 665, Lane Cove, NSW 2066

British Library Cataloguing in Publication Data
Konior, Mary
 Crochet lace
 1. Crocheting
 I. Title
 746.434
 ISBN 0-7137-2212-6

Typeset by Litho Link Ltd, Welshpool, Powys, Wales
Printed and bound in Great Britain by Butler &
Tanner Ltd

Contents

rochet is a seductive medium that has hooked many; 'just one more stitch' is a well-known siren call. Surprisingly, there is no machine capable of reproducing crochet in the way that knitting is fabricated by machinery. Crochet just *has* to be handmade.

The work divides naturally into two types: decorative cotton crochet, which is comparable to bobbin or needlepoint lace, and utilitarian wool crochet, which is comparable to knitting. Wool crochet can be further subdivided into close-textured solid fabrics and open-textured lace fabrics. The latter are not well known, and, as they are so attractive and deserve to be more widely appreciated, I decided to record them in this book.

First and foremost, they should be regarded as a type of lace. That these fabrics are wearable and are made with a hook are secondary factors and a bonus. They are the equivalent of the Shetland knitted laces, and they developed historically as shawl designs, partly because the overall shape of the fabric needed to be simple in order to accommodate the visually complex patterns, and partly because their development coincided with the fashion for wearing shawls that sprang up in Victorian times.

The art of decorative cotton crochet had begun to flourish during the latter half of the eighteenth century, especially in France, and by the mid-nineteenth century it had become a sophisticated and well-established drawing-room pursuit in Britain. There was, however, also a background tradition of rustic cottage work running concurrently with the more genteel art.

The memoirs of Elizabeth Grant, of Rothiemurchus in Inverness-shire, recall an occasion in 1812 when Elizabeth watched an old aunt engaged in crochet: 'It was done with a little hook which she manufactured for herself out of the tooth of an old tortoiseshell comb, and she used to go on looping her home-spun wool as quick as fingers could move.' (*Memoirs of a Highland Lady*, ed.

Angus Davidson, John Murray, 1950.)

It is from the lowly cottage crochet that the classic lace fabric patterns first began to develop. They were permutations of the basic stitches that a worker could devise for herself by counting stitches and spaces, either singly or in groups, and even though the interchange of these elements could result in apparently complex patterns, they were easily worked by eye.

A typical example of unsophisticated cottage work is the treble-block structure, which became known as the Cottage Shawl or Charity Shawl pattern. It was a favourite for charity purposes not only because it was easy to make (it is still, often, the first pattern attempted by beginners when learning to crochet), but also because it was an ideal medium for rainbow work, which was a euphemism for the use of multi-coloured scraps of wool.

The Cottage Shawl was so common during the mid- and late Victorian periods that it almost merits the status of national dress. A sturdy outdoor version, often made in a serviceable grey with a scarlet border, was well in evidence in industrial, agricultural and fishing communities in England as a work shawl. The frontispiece, from a plate by the nineteenth-century photographer Frank Meadow Sutcliffe, of a group of fishergirls on the quay at Whitby, Yorkshire, shows the girl on the left apparently making such a shawl, while the two next to her wear theirs as head shawls.

Another easy-to-make structure is the basic shell pattern, which still ranks as beginner's work, and it is reasonable to suppose from its inherent simplicity that this, too, was an early form of cottage crochet. However, it is possible that, historically, the first lace fabric was an unadorned chain net, for there are several early and enigmatic references to 'chain lace'.

There are well-documented examples of chain net, treble net, treble-block and shell patterns dating back from the 1840s to 1850s, but it is difficult to assess exactly when the more ornate crochet lace fabrics evolved. Most were fully developed and in common use by the 1880s, judging by the frequent appearance of such designs in women's publications of the period. Some very elaborate combinations of patterns were lavished on shawls made for special occasions – for weddings, anniversaries or christenings – and such shawls were, and still are, treasured according to the degree of stamina and skill involved in their making. Sadly, in the Victorian age of high infant mortality, christening shawls must sometimes have served as shrouds.

Although the classic crochet lace fabrics evolved as shawl designs, there is no reason why they should not now be used as a basis for design in other spheres. They could, for example, be adapted for table-cloths or wall hangings or even for any simply shaped garment such as the modern T-shirt. In the 1920s there was a fashion, which now looks strangely modern, for crochet jumpers in artificial silk, planned as simple T shapes. While intricate garment shaping is feasible with the small lace patterns, it is not recommended for larger and more complex laces, as it would be a pity to confuse or distort their character.

The collection of pattern samples in Part I of this book constitutes a vocabulary, and it will be obvious that there is potential for expansion beyond the variations suggested. Many subtle nuances and inflections can follow from a change of mathematical ratio or from the substitution of an alternative basic stitch. However, no collection can claim to be fully comprehensive, and these patterns have been selected on the basis of their technical practicality as well as their decorative allure. The collection of shawls in Part II demonstrates how compatible some patterns are, and how successfully two or three different examples can be combined.

Enthusiasts may wonder why filet crochet and Irish crochet patterns have been omitted. The reason is that traditionally these were regarded as decorative cotton laces, rather than as wool fabrics, and so they fall outside the scope of this study.

The shawls have been selected to suit a worker of average technical ability and experience; none is excessively difficult to make – indeed the Cottage Shawls can safely be attempted by a novice once the treble stitch has been mastered. Part II also includes advice on the preliminary planning necessary for working the different structural forms of square, circular and triangular shawls in the hope that readers will be encouraged to be adventurous and to create original designs for themselves.

PART I

A Collection of Lace Fabric Patterns

'Your mother was not brought up right,' her aunt snapped. 'What does she know about crocheting. She doesn't know star stitch from coffee-bean stitch . . .'

The Mary Frances Knitting and Crocheting Book
Jane Eayre Fryer, 1919

STITCHES AND ABBREVIATIONS

Symbol	UK/Australia/ Canada	US
o	chain (ch)	chain
•	slipstitch (ss)	slipstitch
+	double crochet (dc)	single crochet
T	treble (tr)	double crochet
F	double treble (dtr)	treble or triple crochet
A	2 treble together (2tr-tog)	2 double crochet together
①	puff stitch of 3 half-tr	puff stitch of 3 half dc
①	puff stitch of 4 half-tr	puff stitch of 4 half dc
⊗	picot	picot

The diagrams have been planned so that their layout relates visually to the crochet fabric as far as possible, with a consistent relationship between the symbols. However, there are examples where these have had to be distorted for the sake of pattern clarity. Once the worker is familiar with the symbols, it should be clear where each foundation chain begins. The turning chains indicate the direction of a particular row.

FOUNDATION CHAINS

There is no need to count a foundation chain carefully when working in rows. Instead, make a chain longer than necessary and leave the excess unused when working the first row. Afterwards, the excess chain can be cut off, leaving just a short length to be unpicked and the yarn darned in. It is assumed that workers will adopt this method when experimenting with the patterns given, and for this reason the exact number of chains for each foundation is not specified.

TENSION

Notice that tension is loose in the samples shown – much looser than would be considered correct for close-textured crochet. These samples were worked in 2-ply lace yarns, using hook sizes 4.00mm or 4.50mm (US sizes F and G). They were also 'dressed' in preparation for photography. Dressing, an essential finishing process that can stretch lace fabrics considerably, is explained in Part II.

PATTERN NAMES

The names are generally descriptive and intended solely to distinguish one pattern from another. No further significance should be attributed to them unless a specific reason is given. In crochet there is no standardization of names, other than those of the basic stitches, and old publications often yield several different names for the same pattern.

WORKING IN ROUNDS

The samples shown were worked in rows, and the pattern directions are, therefore, given in rows. The majority can also be worked in rounds without difficulty, but a few, notably the asymmetric 'crazy' patterns, are not suitable for working in this way unless the work is turned in direction after every round.

'We had to sit quiet and crochet, till the evening was over and then Alice came to our room, much agitated and we told Papa.'

Queen Victoria, a letter to the Princess Royal, December 1860 (*Dearest Child*, ed. Roger Fulford, Evans Brothers Ltd, 1964)

The royal ladies calmed their nerves with crochet while an agitated Princess Alice received a proposal of marriage from Prince Louis of Hesse. Annoyingly, the Queen omitted details of her crochet work, but perhaps it would have been something relevant to Alice's not unexpected betrothal.

Foundation chain as required.

1st row: 3tr into 4th ch from hook, *miss 3ch, 4tr into next ch. Repeat from * for the length required, 3ch, turn.

2nd row: 4tr between 2nd and 3rd tr of first shell, *4tr between 2nd and 3rd tr of next shell. Repeat from * to end of row, 3ch, turn. Repeat 2nd row as required.

Variations

1. The shells can be enlarged with extra trebles.
2. The shells can be worked into the top of a treble instead of between trebles.

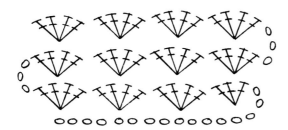

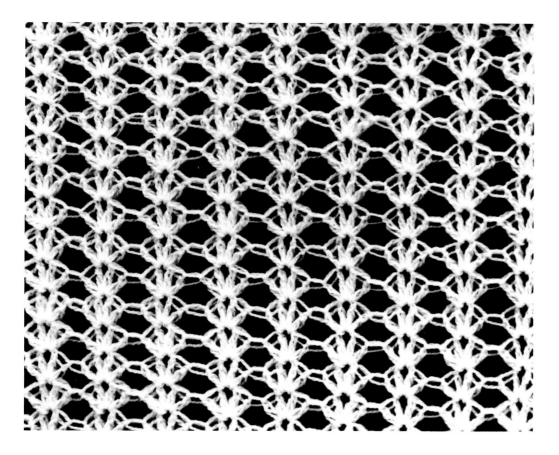

Foundation chain as required.
1st row: (1tr, 1ch, 2tr) into 4th ch from hook, *miss 4ch, (2tr, 1ch, 2tr) into next ch. Repeat from * for the length required, 3ch, turn.
2nd row: (2tr, 1ch, 2tr) into first 1ch space, *(2tr, 1ch, 2tr) into next 1ch space. Repeat from * to end of row, 3ch, turn.
Repeat 2nd row as required.

Variations

1. The shells can be expanded further by working 1ch between every treble.
2. Substitute (3tr, 2ch, 3tr) for (2tr, 1ch, 2tr).

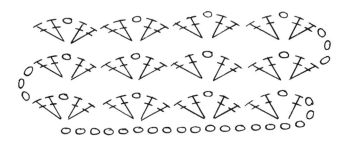

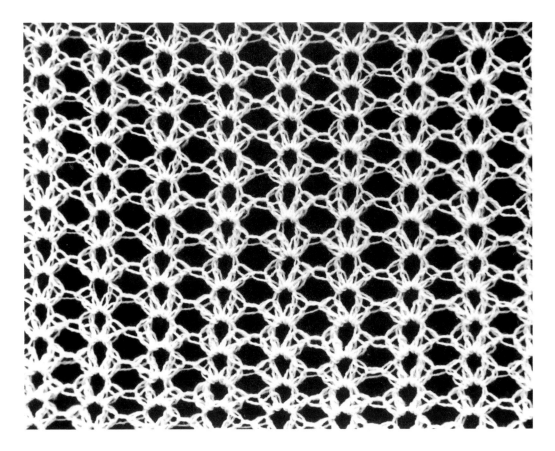

Foundation chain as required.

1st row: 3tr into 4th ch from hook, *1ch, miss 2ch of foundation, 1dc into next ch, 1ch, miss 2ch of foundation, 4tr into next ch. Repeat from * for the length required, 3ch, turn.

2nd row: 4tr between 2nd and 3rd tr of first shell, *1ch, 1dc into next dc, 1ch, 4tr between 2nd and 3rd tr of next shell. Repeat from * to end of row, 3ch, turn.

Repeat 2nd row as required.

Variations

1. The bar can be altered by substituting a treble for each double crochet.
2. The shells can be enlarged with extra trebles.
3. The chains can be increased in length.

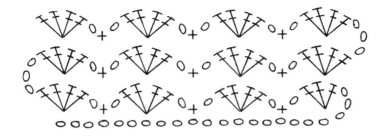

Foundation chain as required.

1st row: 4tr into 4th ch from hook, *miss 2ch, 1dc into next ch, miss 2ch, 5tr into next ch. Repeat from * for the length required, 3ch, turn.

2nd row: 1dc into 3rd tr of first shell, *5tr into next dc, 1dc into 3rd tr of next shell. Repeat from * to end of row, 3ch, turn.

3rd row: 5tr into first dc, *1dc into 3rd tr of next shell, 5tr into next dc. Repeat from * to end of row, 3ch, turn.

Repeat 2nd and 3rd rows as required.

Variation

A treble can be substituted for the double crochet and the turning chain adjusted.

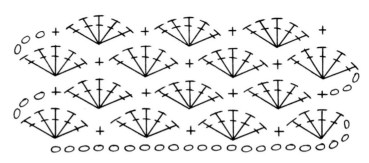

Foundation chain as required.

1st row: 3tr into 4th ch from hook, *miss 3ch, 4tr into next ch. Repeat from * for the length required, 3ch, turn.

2nd row: (1tr, 2ch, 1tr) between 2nd and 3rd tr of first shell, *(1tr, 2ch, 1tr) between 2nd and 3rd tr of next shell. Repeat from * to end of row, 3ch, turn.

3rd row: 4tr into first 2ch space, *4tr into next 2ch space. Repeat from * to end of row, 3ch, turn.

Repeat 2nd and 3rd rows as required.

Variation

The shells and triangles can be aligned vertically instead of horizontally.

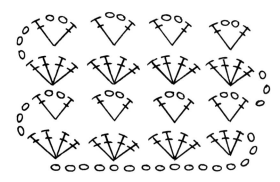

Variation showing vertical alignment

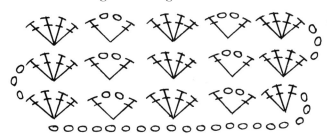

Foundation chain as required.

1st row: 5tr into 4th ch from hook, *miss 4ch, (1tr, 2ch, 1tr) into next ch, miss 4ch, 6tr into next ch. Repeat from * for the length required, 3ch, turn.

2nd row: (1tr, 2ch, 1tr) between 3rd and 4th tr of first shell, *6tr into next 2ch space, (1tr, 2ch, 1tr) between 3rd and 4th tr of next shell. Repeat from * to end or row, 3ch, turn.

3rd row: 6tr into first 2ch space, *(1tr, 2ch, 1tr) between 3rd and 4th tr of next shell, 6tr into next 2ch space. Repeat from * to end of row, 3ch, turn.

Repeat 2nd and 3rd rows as required.

Variations

1. The shells can be reduced to 4 trebles.
2. Double trebles can be substituted for the shell trebles, and the turning chains adjusted accordingly.

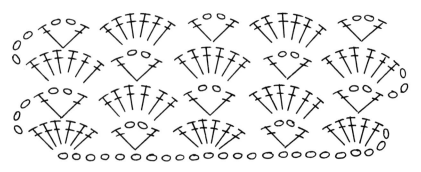

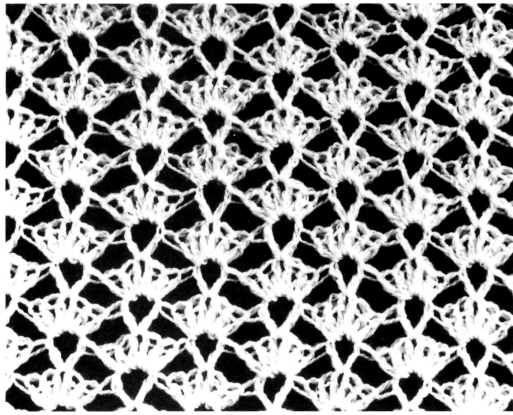

Foundation chain as required.

1st row: (1tr, 1dc) into 4th ch from hook, *miss 2ch, (2tr, 1dc) into next ch. Repeat from * for the length required, 3ch, turn.

2nd row: (1tr, 1dc) into first dc, *(2tr, 1dc) into next dc. Repeat from * to end of row, 3ch, turn.

Repeat 2nd row as required.

Variation

Each 2tr can be drawn together as if decreasing.

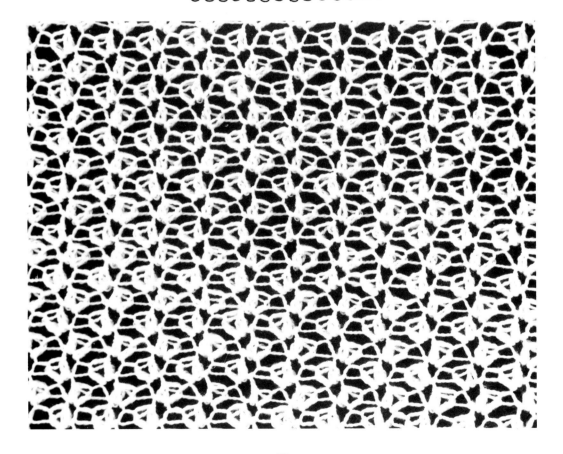

Also known as *Five Stitch, Daisy Stitch* and *Point Neige*. Some Weldon's patterns of the 1880s confusingly called it *Shell Stitch*.

Foundation chain as required.

1st row: miss first ch, (insert hook into next ch and draw yarn through) 5 times, yarn-over-hook, draw through all loops, *1ch, insert hook into eye of star just made and draw yarn through, insert hook into back of last loop of star and draw yarn through, insert hook into last foundation ch used for the star and draw yarn through, (insert hook into next founda-tion ch and draw yarn through) twice, yarn-over-hook and draw through all loops. Repeat from * for the length required, 1ch, 1dc into next foundation ch, 3ch, turn.

2nd row: miss first ch, (insert hook into next ch and draw yarn through) twice, insert hook into dc and draw yarn through, insert hook into eye of next star and draw yarn through, insert hook into next loop along row and draw yarn through, yarn-over-hook and draw through all loops, *1ch, insert hook into eye of star just made and draw yarn through, insert hook into back of last loop of star and draw yarn through, insert hook into same place as last loop of star and draw yarn through, insert hook into eye of next star and draw yarn through, insert hook into next loop along row and draw yarn through, yarn-over-hook and draw through all loops. Repeat from *, ending with 1ch, 1dc into extreme end of row, 3ch, turn.

Repeat 2nd row as required.

Variation

The number of loops in each star can be varied.

The construction of star stitch. (The usual symbols are inappropriate for this pattern.)

Foundation chain as required.

1st row: triangle of (1tr, 1ch, 1tr) into 4th ch from hook, *miss 2ch, triangle of (1tr, 1ch, 1tr) into next ch. Repeat from * for the length required, 3ch, turn.

2nd row: miss first triangle, (1tr, 1ch, 1tr) into space between first and second triangles, *(1tr, 1ch, 1tr) into next space between triangles. Repeat from * to end of row, ending with (1tr, 1ch, 1tr) into space formed by turning ch, 3ch, turn.

Repeat 2nd row as required.

Variations

1. Each triangle can be formed of (1tr, 2ch, 1tr).
2. The triangles can be aligned vertically.

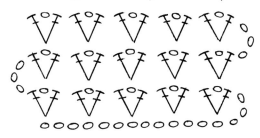

Variation 2, showing vertical alignment

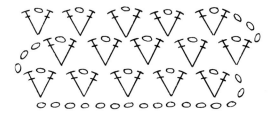

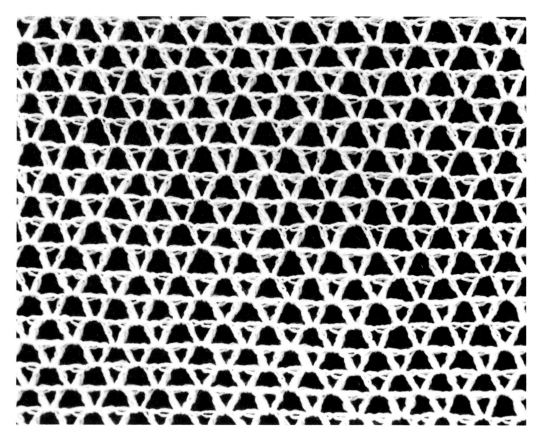

Foundation chain as required.

1st row: 1tr into 8th ch from hook, *2ch, miss 3ch of foundation, 1dc into next ch, 2ch, miss 3ch of foundation, (1tr, 5ch, 1tr) into next ch. Repeat from * for the length required, ending with 1dc, 8ch, turn.

2nd row: 1tr into first dc, *2ch, 1dc into next 5ch loop, 2ch, (1tr, 5ch, 1tr) into next dc. Repeat from *, ending with 1dc into last chain loop, 8ch, turn.

Repeat 2nd row as required.

Variation

The 2ch loops can be lengthened.

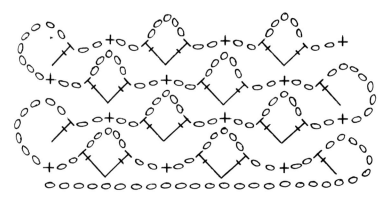

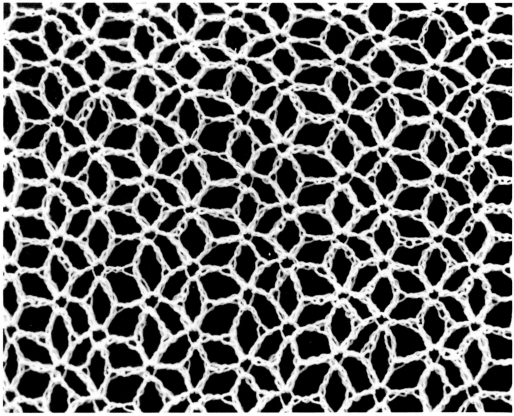

Foundation chain as required.

1st row: 1dc into 9th ch from hook, (1dc into next ch) twice, *3ch, miss 3ch of foundation, 1tr into next ch, 3ch, miss 3ch of foundation, (1dc into next ch) 3 times. Repeat from * for the length required, ending with 2dc instead of 3dc, 6ch, turn.

2nd row: 1dc into first 3ch space, 1dc into first tr, 1dc into next 3ch space, *3ch, 1tr into centre of 3dc, 3ch, 1dc into next space, 1dc into next tr, 1dc into following space. Repeat from * to end of row, ending with 2dc into last space, 6ch, turn.

Repeat 2nd row as required.

Variation

The group of 3dc can be reduced, leaving the centre dc only.

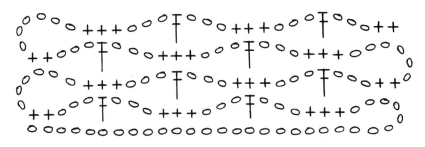

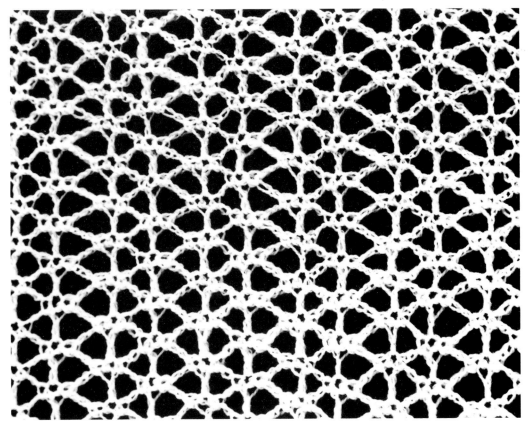

A pattern from *Weldon's Practical Needle-work*, No. 207, published in 1903.

Foundation chain as required.
1st row: (1tr, 1ch, 1tr) into 5th ch from hook, *3ch, miss 4ch of foundation, 1dtr into next ch, 3ch, miss 4ch of foundation, (1tr, 1ch) 3 times into next ch, 1tr into same place. Repeat from * for the length required, ending with 3ch, 1dtr, 1ch, turn.
2nd row: 1dc into first dtr, *3ch, 1dc into next 1ch space, 3ch, (1dc, 3ch, 1dc) into next 1ch space, 3ch, 1dc into following 1ch space, 3ch, 1dc into next dtr. Repeat from *, ending with 3ch, 1dc into next 1ch space, 3ch, 1dc into 4ch space at end, 9ch, turn.
3rd row: *(1tr, 1ch) 3 times into dc-over-dtr,

1tr into same place, 3ch, 1dtr into centre chain space above next fan, 3ch. Repeat from *, ending with (1tr, 1ch) twice into dc at end of row, 1tr into same place, 3ch, turn.
4th row: 1dc into first 1ch space, 3ch, 1dc into next 1ch space, *3ch, 1dc into next dtr, 3ch, 1dc into next 1ch space, 3ch, (1dc, 3ch, 1dc) into next 1ch space, 3ch, 1dc into following 1ch space. Repeat from *, ending with 3ch, 1dc into 4th of 9ch at end, 4ch, turn.
5th row: (1tr, 1ch, 1tr) into first dc, *3ch, 1dtr into centre chain space above next fan, 3ch, (1tr, 1ch) 3 times into dc-over-dtr, 1tr into same place. Repeat from *, ending with 3ch, 1dtr into last space, 1ch, turn.
Repeat 2nd to 5th rows as required.

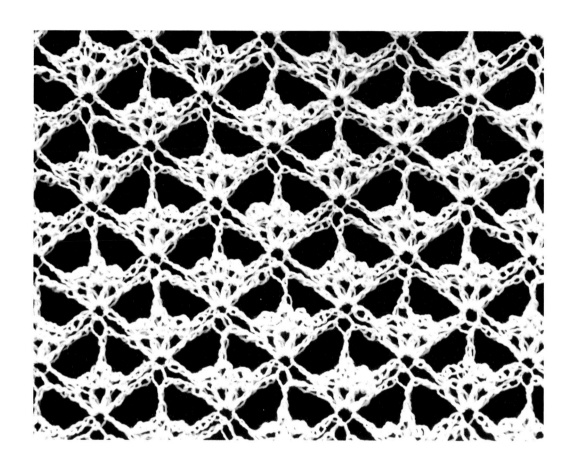

Foundation chain as required.

1st row: 1dc into 8th ch from hook, *miss 2ch of foundation, 5tr into next ch, miss 2ch of foundation, 1dc into next ch, 5ch, miss 5ch of foundation, 1dc into next ch. Repeat from * for the length required, 8ch, turn.

2nd row: 1dc into 3rd ch of first loop, *5ch, 1dc into centre tr of shell, 5ch, 1dc into 3rd ch of next loop. Repeat from * to end of row, 3ch, turn.

3rd row: 5tr into first dc, 1dc into 3rd ch of first loop, *5ch, 1dc into 3rd ch of next loop, 5tr into next dc, 1dc into 3rd ch of next loop. Repeat from * to end of row, 8ch, turn.

4th row: *1dc into centre tr of next shell, 5ch, 1dc into 3rd ch of next loop, 5ch. Repeat from *, ending with 1dc into last shell, 8ch, turn.

5th row: 1dc into 3rd ch of first loop, *5tr into next dc, 1dc into 3rd ch of next loop, 5ch, 1dc into 3rd ch of next loop. Repeat from * to end of row, 8ch, turn.

Repeat 2nd to 5th rows as required.

Variations

1. The shells can be arranged in a different sequence.
2. The double crochet can be worked into each loop instead of into the chain stitch.

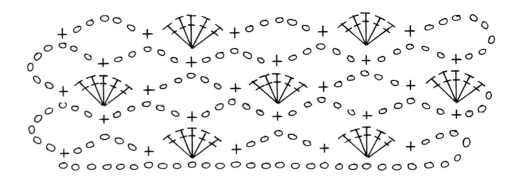

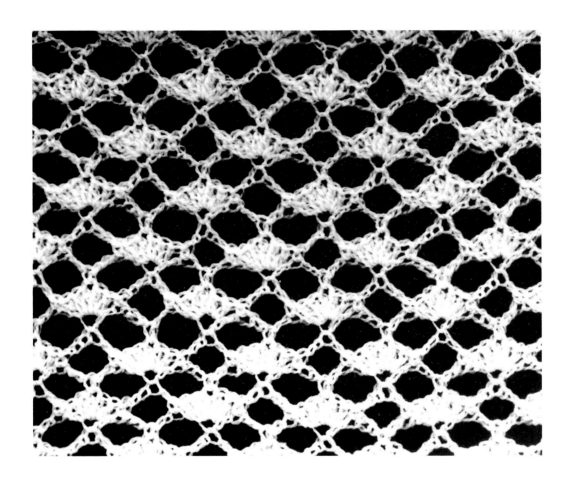

Foundation chain as required.

1st row: 1dc into 10th ch from hook, *2ch, miss 2ch of foundation, (1tr into next ch) 4 times, 2ch, miss 2ch of foundation, 1dc into next ch, 5ch, miss 5ch of foundation, 1dc into next ch. Repeat from * for the length required, ending with 2ch, 4tr, turn.

2nd row: *5ch, 1dc into next 2ch space, 2ch, 4tr into next 5ch space, 2ch, 1dc into next 2ch space. Repeat from *, ending with 4tr into last space, turn.

Repeat 2nd row as required.

Variations

1. The lengths of chain and number of trebles in each block can be varied.

2. A row of blocks can be alternated with a row of chains.

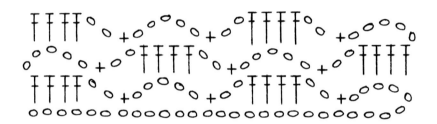

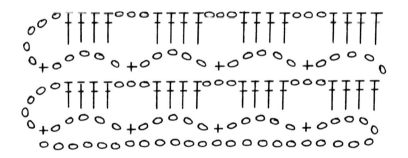

Variation 2, showing alternate rows of blocks and chains

This is the basic treble-block pattern embellished with spiders.

Foundation chain as required.
1st row: miss 7ch, *(1tr into next ch) 3 times, 2ch, miss 2ch of foundation. Repeat from * for the length required, but the total number of blocks should be divisible by three. Work 1tr in order to end the row with a space, 3ch, turn.
2nd row: 2tr into first space, *2ch, 3tr into next space, 6ch, 3tr into next space, 2ch, 3tr into next space. Repeat from * to end of row, 5ch, turn.
3rd row: *3tr into next 2ch space, 8ch, miss 6ch space, 3tr into following 2ch space, 2ch. Repeat from *, ending with 1tr at end of row, 3ch, turn.
4th row: 2tr into first 2ch space, *12ch, miss 8ch space, 3tr into following 2ch space.

Repeat from * to end of row, 5ch, turn.
5th row: *3tr into 12ch space, 4ch, 1dc under the 6ch, 8ch and 12ch loops to connect them together, 4ch, 3tr into 12ch space, 2ch. Repeat from *, ending with 1tr at end of row, 3ch, turn.
6th row: 2tr into first 2ch space, *2ch, 3tr into 4ch space, 2ch, 3tr into next 4ch space, 2ch, 3tr into next space. Repeat from * to end of row, 5ch, turn.
7th row: *3tr into next space, 2ch. Repeat from *, ending with 1tr at end of row, 3ch, turn.
Repeat 2nd to 7th rows as required.

Variations
1. The spiders can be arranged in a different sequence.
2. The spiders can be enlarged by making extra chains and solid centres.

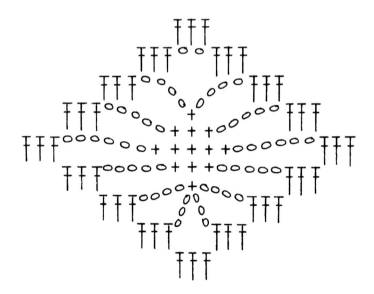

Variation 2, showing an enlarged spider

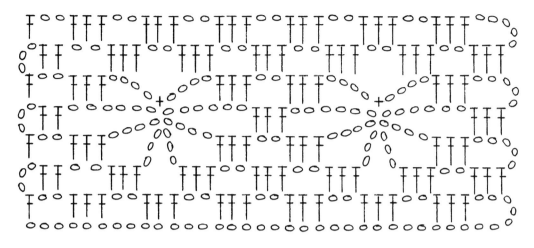

Foundation chain as required.

1st row: 1tr into 4th ch from hook, 1tr into next ch, *2ch, miss 2ch of foundation, (1tr into next ch) 3 times. Repeat from * for the length required, 3ch, turn.

2nd row: *(2tr, 2ch, 2tr) into next 2ch space. Repeat from * to end of row, 1tr into top of turning ch, 5ch, turn.

3rd row: *3tr into next 2ch space, 2ch. Repeat from * to end of row, 1tr into top of turning ch, 5ch, turn.

4th row: 2tr into first 2ch space, *(2tr, 2ch, 2tr) into next 2ch space. Repeat from *, ending with (2tr, 2ch, 1tr) into 5ch space, 3ch, turn.

5th row: 2tr into first 2ch space, *2ch, 3tr into next 2ch space. Repeat from *, ending in last 5ch space, 3ch, turn.

Repeat 2nd to 5th rows as required.

Variation

Substitute (3tr, 2ch, 3tr) for (2tr, 2ch, 2tr) in the 2nd and 4th rows, and substitute 4tr for the 3tr in the 1st, 3rd and 5th rows.

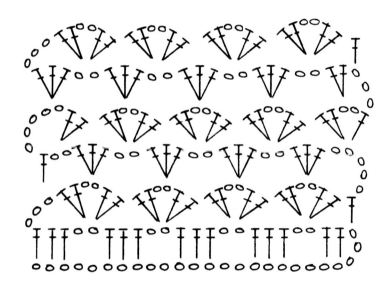

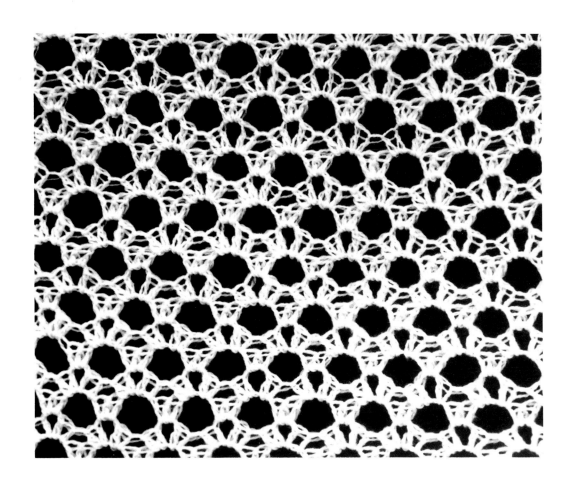

Foundation chain as required.

1st row: 1dc into 4th ch from hook, (1dc into next ch) twice, *3ch, miss 3ch of foundation, (1dc into next ch) 3 times. Repeat from * for the length required, ending with 2dc instead of 3dc, 1ch, turn.

2nd row: 1dc into first dc, *5tr into next 3ch space, 1dc into 2nd dc. Repeat from *, ending with 3tr into final space, 1ch, turn.

3rd row: 1dc into first tr, 1dc into next tr, *3ch, 1dc into 2nd tr of next group, (1dc into next tr) twice. Repeat from *, ending with 1ch,

1tr into final dc, 3ch, turn.

4th row: 2tr into first 1ch space, *1dc into 2nd dc, 5tr into next 3ch space. Repeat from *, ending with 1dc into last dc, 4ch, turn.

5th row: *1dc into 2nd tr of next group, (1dc into next tr) twice, 3ch. Repeat from *, ending with 2dc instead of 3dc, 1ch, turn.

Repeat 2nd to 5th rows as required.

Variation
The 5tr groups can be enlarged, and the 3ch loops made correspondingly longer.

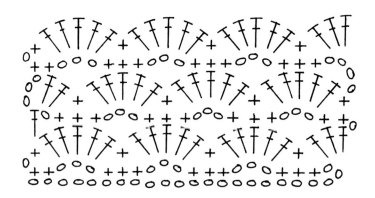

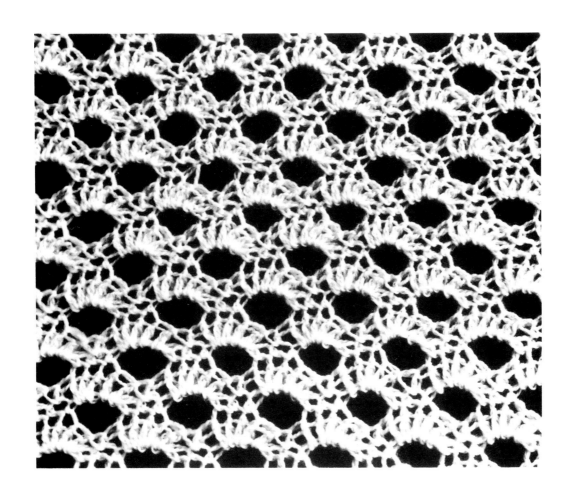

Also known as *Crazy Stitch*, the asymmetric, alternating blocks were frequently described as 'crazy'. This version is lacier than the better known, traditional *Crazy Stitch*.

Foundation chain as required.
1st row: 1tr into 4th ch from hook, (1tr into next ch) twice, 2ch, 1tr into same place as previous tr, *miss 3ch of foundation, (1tr into next ch) 4 times, 2ch, 1tr into same place as previous tr. Repeat from * for the length required, 3ch, turn.
2nd row: (3tr, 2ch, 1tr) into first 2ch space, *(4tr, 2ch, 1tr) into next 2ch space. Repeat from * to end of row, 3ch, turn.
Repeat 2nd row as required.

Variation

For traditional *Crazy Stitch* reduce each block by 1tr and substitute a double crochet for the single treble throughout, which results in a closer fabric. This was once a favourite Victorian stitch for square baby shawls as all edges are neatly serrated and need no decoration apart from a bobble edging, as given for the Cottage Shawl (see page 88).

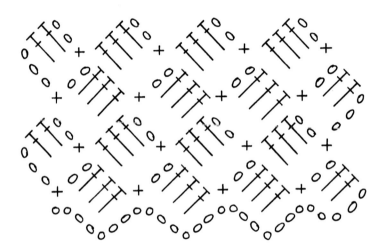

Variation showing traditional Crazy Stitch

Foundation chain as required.

1st row: 4dtr into 5th ch from hook, *miss 4ch of foundation, 5dtr into next ch. Repeat from * for the length required, 5ch, turn.

2nd row: *5dtr between 4th and 5th dtr of next fan. Repeat from * to end of row, 5ch, turn.

Repeat 2nd row as required.

Variations

1. The number of double trebles in each fan can be increased.

2. Trebles can be substituted for double trebles throughout and the turning chains adjusted to correspond.

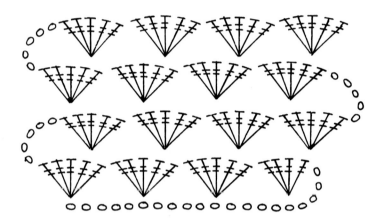

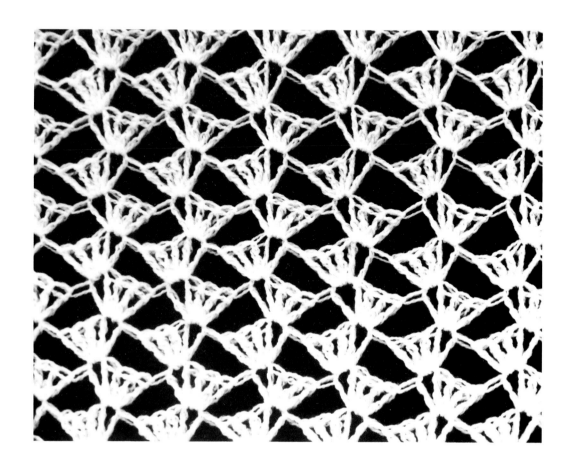

Foundation chain as required.

1st row: 2dtr into 5th ch from hook, *miss 2ch, 1dc into next ch, miss 2ch, 5dtr into next ch. Repeat from * for the length required, ending with 1dc, 4ch, turn.

2nd row: 2dtr into first dc, *1dc into centre dtr of next fan, 5dtr into next dc. Repeat from *, ending with 1dc into top of turning chain, 4ch, turn.

Repeat 2nd row as required.

Variations

1. The number of double trebles in each fan can be increased to seven.

2. The layout easily adapts to a triangular form, which was a favourite Victorian method for making a 'fascinator' or small head shawl, often bobble-edged and worn, fascinatingly, with the point over the forehead. The version shown is from *Mrs Leach's Fancy Work Basket*, 1886.

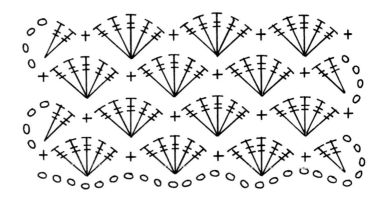

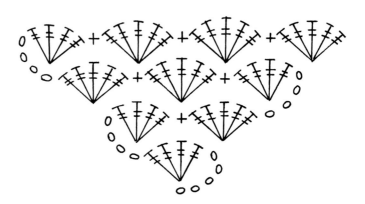

Variation 2, showing a triangular layout

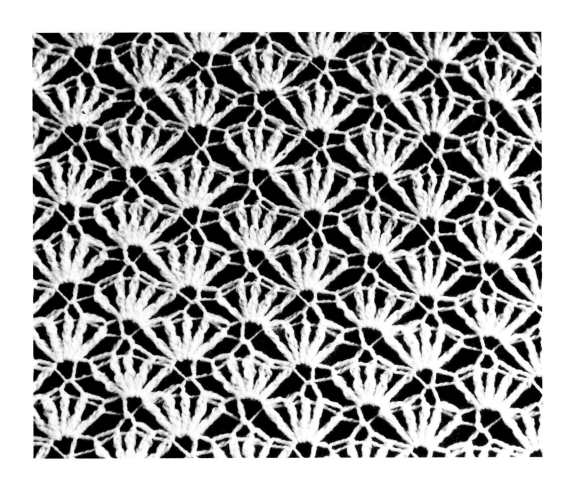

Foundation chain as required.

1st row: 2tr into 6th ch from hook, *miss 2ch, (1tr into next ch) 8 times, miss 2ch, (2tr, 2ch, 2tr) into next ch. Repeat from * for the length required, ending with (2tr, 2ch, 1tr), 4ch, turn.

2nd row: 3dtr into first space, *(2tr, 2ch, 2tr) into 4th of 8tr, 8dtr into next 2ch space. Repeat from *, ending with 4dtr into last space, 3ch, turn.

3rd row: miss first dtr, (1tr into next dtr) 3 times, *(2tr, 2ch, 2tr) into next 2ch space, (1tr into next dtr) 8 times. Repeat from *, ending

with 4tr instead of 8tr, 5ch, turn.

4th row: 2tr into first tr, *8dtr into next 2ch space, (2tr, 2ch, 2tr) into 4th of 8tr. Repeat from *, ending with (2tr, 2ch, 1tr), 5ch, turn.

5th row: 2tr into first space, *(1tr into next dtr) 8 times, (2tr, 2ch, 2tr) into next 2ch space. Repeat from *, ending with (2tr, 2ch, 1tr), 4ch, turn.

Repeat 2nd to 5th rows as required.

Variation

The shells can be reduced to triangles of (1tr, 2ch, 1tr).

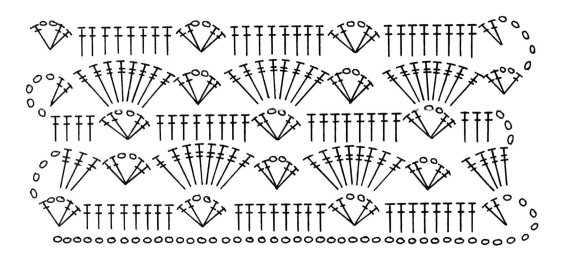

Foundation chain as required.

1st row: 1dc into 2nd ch from hook, *2ch, miss 2ch of foundation, (1tr, 2ch, 1tr) into next ch, 2ch, miss 2ch of foundation, 1dc into next ch. Repeat from * for the length required, 1ch, turn.

2nd row: 1dc into first dc, *5dtr into centre of next triangle, 1dc into next dc. Repeat from * to end of row, 5ch, turn.

3rd row: 1tr into first dc, *2ch, 1dc into 3rd of 5dtr, 2ch, (1tr, 2ch, 1tr) into next dc. Repeat from * to end of row, 4ch, turn.

4th row: 2dtr into first triangle, *1dc into next dc, 5dtr into next triangle. Repeat from *, ending with 3dtr into last triangle, 1ch, turn.

5th row: 1dc into first dtr, *2ch, (1tr, 2ch, 1tr) into next dc, 2ch, 1dc into 3rd of 5dtr. Repeat from *, ending with 1dc, 1ch, turn.

Repeat 2nd to 5th rows as required.

Variations

1. Substitute 7dtr for each 5dtr fan.
2. Trebles can be substituted for double trebles throughout, and the turning chains adjusted to correspond.

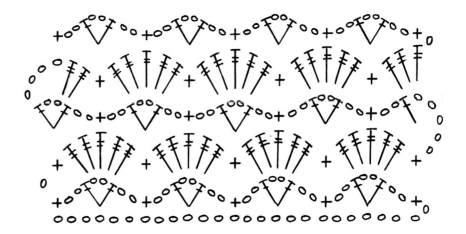

Foundation chain as required.

1st row: 4dtr into 5th ch from hook, *miss 3ch, 1tr into next ch, miss 3ch, 9dtr into next ch. Repeat from * for the length required, ending with 5dtr instead of 9dtr, 4ch, turn.

2nd row: 1tr into 2nd dtr, 1ch, 1tr into 4th dtr, 1ch, *1tr into next tr, 1ch, (miss 1dtr, 1tr into next dtr, 1ch) 4 times. Repeat from *, ending with 1tr into last dtr, 3ch, turn.

3rd row: *9dtr into tr-over-tr, 1tr into centre space over fan. Repeat from *, ending with 1tr into last space, 4ch, turn.

4th row: *(miss 1dtr, 1tr into next dtr, 1ch) 4 times, 1tr into tr, 1ch. Repeat from *, ending with 1tr into top of turning ch, 4ch, turn.

5th row: 4dtr into first tr, *1tr into centre space over fan, 9dtr into tr-over-tr. Repeat from *, ending with 5dtr instead of 9dtr, 4ch, turn.

Repeat 2nd to 5th rows as required.

Variation

Substitute 7tr for each 9dtr fan, adjusting the crown to correspond.

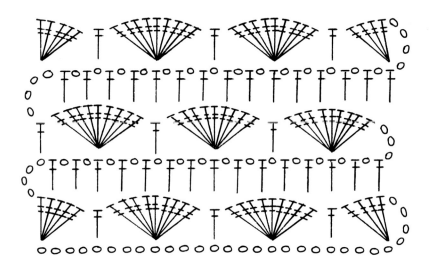

Foundation chain as required.

1st row: 1tr into 7th ch from hook, *3ch, miss 3ch of foundation, (1dc into next ch) 5 times, 3ch, miss 3ch of foundation, (1tr, 3ch, 1tr) into next ch. Repeat from * for the length required, 4ch, turn.

2nd row: 4dtr into first space, *1ch, miss next dc, (1dc into following dc) 3 times, 1ch, 9dtr into centre of next triangle. Repeat from *, ending with 5dtr into last space, 1ch, turn.

3rd row: (1dc into next dtr) 3 times, *3ch, (1tr, 3ch, 1tr) into centre of next 3dc, 3ch, miss 2dtr, (1dc into next dtr) 5 times. Repeat from *, ending with 3dc, 1ch, turn.

4th row: (1dc into next dc) twice, *1ch, 9dtr into next triangle, 1ch, miss next dc, (1dc into following dc) 3 times. Repeat from *, ending with 2dc, 6ch, turn.

5th row: 1tr into first dc, *3ch, miss 2dtr, (1dc into next dtr) 5 times, 3ch, (1tr, 3ch, 1tr) into centre of next 3dc. Repeat from *, ending with (1tr, 3ch, 1tr) into last dc, 4ch, turn.

Repeat 2nd to 5th rows as required.

Variations

1. The chains between each fan can be lengthened.
2. Substitute 7tr for 9dtr.

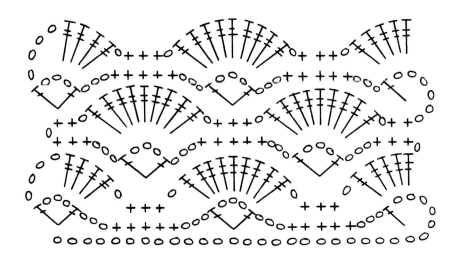

Foundation chain as required.

1st row: 1tr into 6th ch from hook, *1tr into each of next 6ch, miss 2ch, 1tr into each of next 6ch, (1tr, 2ch, 1tr) into following ch. Repeat from * for the length required, 5ch, turn.

2nd row: 1tr into first space, *1tr into each of next 6tr, miss 2tr, 1tr into each of next 6tr, (1tr, 2ch, 1tr) into next space. Repeat from * to end of row, 5ch, turn.

3rd row: as 2nd row.

4th row: 1tr into first space, *1ch, 1tr into next tr, (1ch, miss 1tr, 1tr into next tr) twice, miss 3tr, (1tr into next tr, 1ch, miss 1tr) 3 times, (1tr, 2ch, 1tr) into next space. Repeat from * to end of row, 5ch, turn.

5th row: 1tr into first space, *(1tr into next tr, 1tr into 1ch space) 3 times, miss 2tr, (1tr into 1ch space, 1tr into next tr) 3 times, (1tr, 2ch, 1tr) into next space. Repeat from * to end of row, 5ch, turn.

Repeat 2nd to 5th rows as required.

Variations

1. The number of trebles between each increase and decrease can be altered.

2. The open 4th row can be worked in a different sequence with the plain rows.

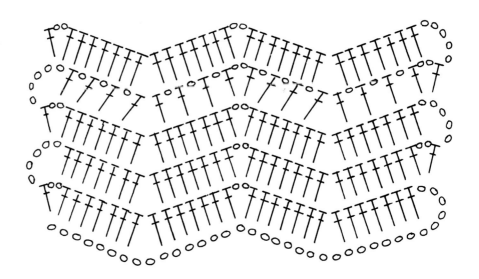

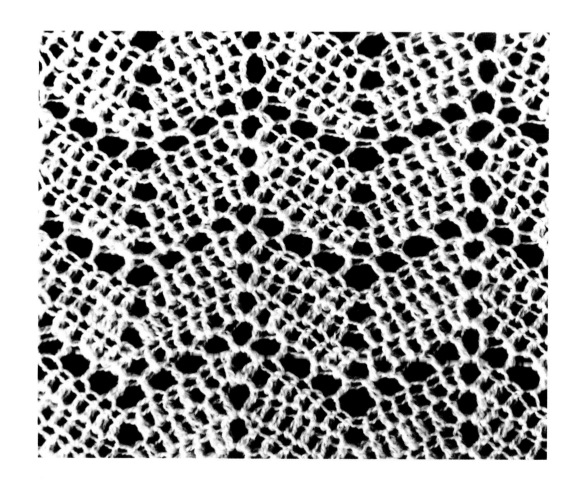

This pattern has a sequence of increases and decreases that resembles a Shetland knitting pattern of the same name.

Foundation chain as required.

1st row: 1tr into 4th ch from hook, *(yarn-over-hook, insert hook in next ch, yarn-over-hook and draw through, yarn-over-hook and draw through 2 loops) twice, yarn-over-hook and draw through 3 remaining loops [= 2tr-tog]. Repeat from * twice more, **(2ch, 1tr into next ch of foundation) 3 times, 2ch, (2tr-tog) 8 times. Repeat from ** for the length required, ending with (2tr-tog) 4 times instead of 8 times, 3ch, turn.

2nd row: miss first stitch, 1tr into next stitch, 2tr-tog into next 2 stitches, *2tr-tog into next 2ch space, 2tr-tog into next tr and next 2ch space, 2ch, 1tr into same space, 2ch, 1tr into next tr, 2ch, 1tr into next space, 2ch, 2tr-tog into same space and next tr, 2tr-tog into next space, (2tr-tog into next 2 stitches) 4 times. Repeat from * to end of row, finishing with (2tr-tog into next 2 stitches) twice instead of 4 times, 3ch, turn.

Repeat 2nd row as required.

Variations

1. The number of 2tr-tog can be altered and the number of 2ch spaces adjusted to correspond.

2. Double trebles can be substituted for trebles throughout, and the turning chains adjusted to correspond.

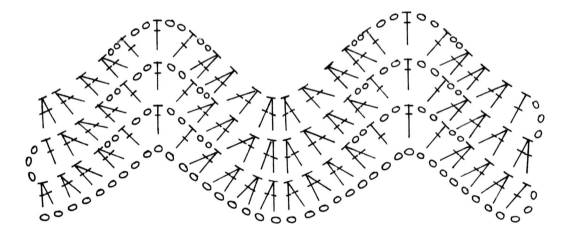

Foundation chain as required.

1st row: 2tr into 6th ch from hook, (2tr into next ch) 3 times, *miss 2ch, 1tr into next ch, miss 2ch, (2tr into next ch) 4 times. Repeat from * for the length required, ending with miss 2ch, 1tr into next ch, 3ch, turn.

2nd row: miss first 3tr, *(2tr into next tr) 4 times, miss 2tr, 1tr into single tr, miss 2tr. Repeat from *, ending with 1tr into top of turning ch, 3ch, turn.

Repeat 2nd row as required.

Variations

1. A short length of chain can be worked before and after the single treble to make a wider panel.
2. Double trebles can be substituted for trebles throughout and the turning chains adjusted to correspond.

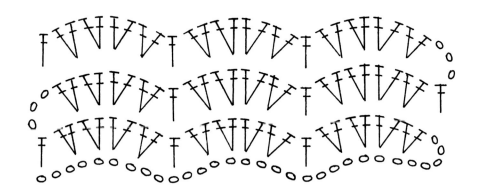

Foundation chain as required.

1st row: 1tr into 4th ch from hook, (2tr into next ch) twice, *2ch, miss 2ch of foundation, 1dc into next ch, 3ch, miss 3ch of foundation, (2tr into next ch) 3 times. Repeat from * for the length required, ending with 2ch, 1dc, 3ch, turn.

2nd row: 6tr into first 2ch space, *2ch, 1dc into 3rd tr of next group, 3ch, 6tr into next 2ch space. Repeat from *, ending with 2ch, 1dc into 3rd tr of last group, 3ch, turn.
Repeat 2nd row as required.

Variations

1. The number of trebles in each group can be varied.
2. The 3ch between each panel can be changed.

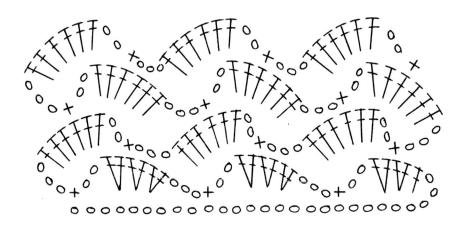

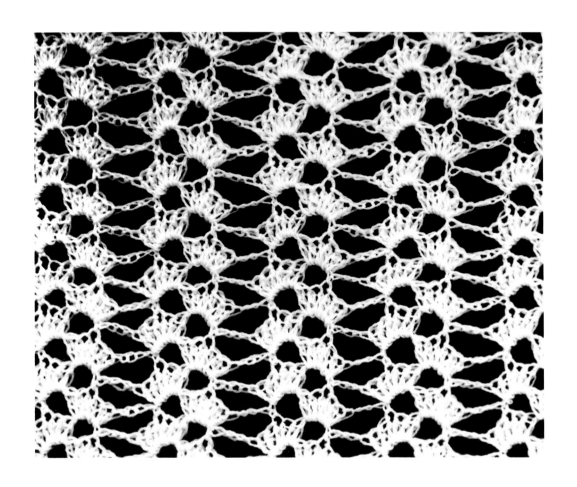

Foundation chain as required.

1st row: 1tr into 4th ch from hook, 1tr into next ch, 4tr into next ch, (1tr into next ch) twice, *miss 3ch of foundation, (1tr into next ch) twice, 4tr into next ch, (1tr into next ch) twice. Repeat from * for the length required, 3ch, turn.

2nd row: *1tr between 2nd and 3rd tr, 1tr between 3rd and 4th tr, 4tr between 4th and 5th tr, 1tr between 5th and 6th tr, 1tr between 6th and 7th tr. Repeat from * in every group to end, 3ch, turn.

Repeat 2nd row as required.

Variations

1. The number of trebles in each feather can be increased.
2. Double trebles can be substituted for trebles throughout and the turning chains adjusted to correspond.

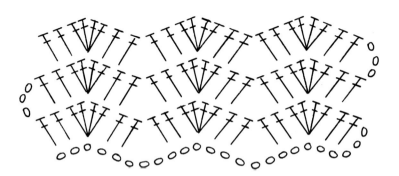

Foundation chain as required.

1st row: 1tr into 5th ch from hook, *1ch, miss 2ch of foundation, (1dtr into next ch) twice, 4dtr into next ch, (1dtr into next ch) twice, 1ch, miss 2ch of foundation, (1tr, 1ch, 1tr) into next ch. Repeat from * for the length required, 4ch, turn.

2nd row: 1tr into first 1ch space, *1ch, miss 1dtr, (1dtr into next dtr) twice, 4dtr into next dtr, (1dtr into next dtr) twice, 1ch, (1tr, 1ch, 1tr) into centre of next bar. Repeat from * to end of row, 4ch, turn.

Repeat 2nd row as required.

Variations

1. The double trebles of each feather can be worked between stitches as shown in the previous pattern, *Feather Panels.*

2. Trebles can be substituted for the double trebles of each feather, and 1dc can be substituted for the (1tr, 1ch, 1tr) bar.

3. The length of the chains between each feather and bar can be increased.

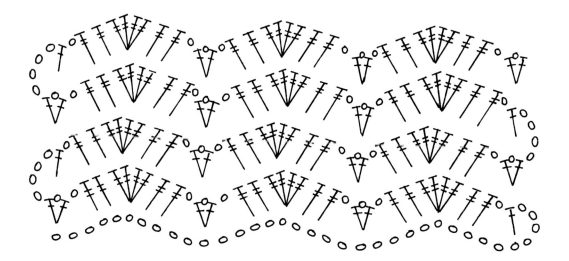

This puff stitch has a variety of other names, including hazel-nut, popcorn, pineapple and bobble stitch. It is also the stitch referred to as 'coffee-bean' on page 9. A puff stitch is, technically, a cluster of loose half-trebles.

Foundation chain as required.

1st row: 1tr into 4th ch from hook, 1tr into next ch, 4tr into next ch, (1tr into next ch) twice, *2ch, miss 3ch of foundation, yarn-over-hook, insert hook into next ch, draw yarn through and draw loop up to the height of a tr, (yarn-over-hook, insert hook into same ch and draw yarn through and up as before) 3 times, yarn-over-hook and draw through all loops [puff made], 2ch, 1 puff into next ch, 2ch, miss 3ch of foundation, (1tr into next ch) twice, 4tr into next ch, (1tr into next ch) twice. Repeat from * for the length required, ending with a feather, 3ch, turn.

2nd row: *1tr between 2nd and 3rd tr, 1tr between 3rd and 4th tr, 4tr between 4th and 5th tr, 1tr between 5th and 6th tr, 1tr between 6th and 7th tr, 2ch, (1 puff, 2ch, 1 puff) between puffs of previous row, 2ch. Repeat from * in every group, ending with a feather, 3ch, turn.

Repeat 2nd row as required.

Variations
1. The number of half-trebles in each puff can be varied.
2. A shell of 4tr can be substituted for each pair of puffs.

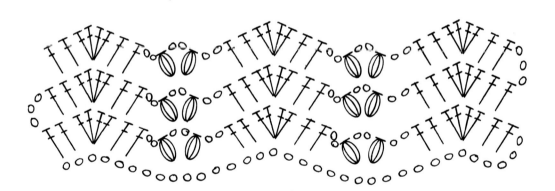

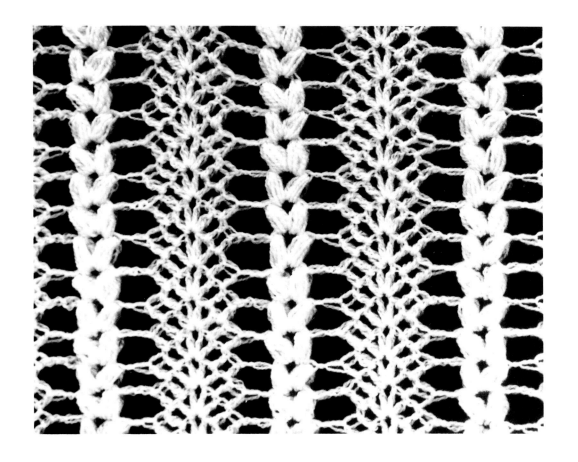

This puff stitch is a cluster of three loose half-trebles.

Foundation chain as required.

1st row: 1dc into 3rd ch from hook, *2ch, miss 2ch of foundation, yarn-over-hook, insert hook into next ch, draw yarn through and draw loop up to the height of a tr, (yarn-over-hook, insert hook into same ch and draw yarn through and up as before) twice, yarn-over-hook and draw through all loops [puff made], 2ch, 1 puff into next ch of foundation, 2ch, miss 2ch of foundation, 1dc into next ch. Repeat from * for the length required, 3ch, turn.

2nd row: 1dc into dc, *2ch, (1 puff, 2ch, 1 puff) into space between next puffs, 2ch, 1dc into next dc. Repeat from * to end, 3ch, turn.

3rd row: *(1 puff, 2ch, 1 puff) into dc, 2ch, 1dc into space between next puffs, 2ch. Repeat from *, ending with (1 puff, 2ch, 1 puff) into last dc, 3ch, turn.

4th row: *(1 puff, 2ch, 1 puff) into space between next puffs, 2ch, 1dc into next dc, 2ch. Repeat from *, ending with (1 puff, 2ch, 1 puff), 3ch, turn.

5th row: *1dc into space between puffs, 2ch, (1 puff, 2ch, 1 puff) into dc, 2ch. Repeat from *, ending with 1dc, 3ch, turn.

Repeat 2nd to 5th rows as required.

Variations

1. The number of half-trebles in each puff can be varied.
2. The length of chain before and after each double crochet can be varied.

PART II

Shawl Designs Using the Patterns

'Barbara clutched her shawl round her and went down
the path in the moonlight.'

East Lynne
Mrs Henry Wood, 1861

SQUARE SHAWLS

There are several well-tried approaches to making crochet shawls. The simplest is to work in rows, backwards and forwards, until a square is completed, then to add an edging around the outside. In theory this is a simple method, but sometimes in practice results are unsatisfactory, for such a form has a tendency to distort if the tension is less than perfect. The foundation may perhaps be tighter or looser than the final row, and the sides, which usually have a great deal of elasticity, can easily become overstretched when an edging is added.

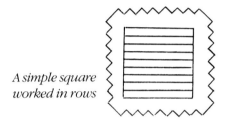

A simple square worked in rows

A more sophisticated way of working in rows is to form a diamond shape, starting at a point, increasing at both sides until the required measurement is achieved and then decreasing to a final point. The four sides thus have a similar degree of elasticity, and, when an edging is added, it is less likely that the entire form will become warped. However, the increases and subsequent decreases must be accurately planned so that they do, in fact, produce a square and not an elongated diamond. Shawls made in this way are said to have been worked diagonally.

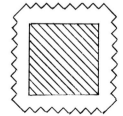

A square worked diagonally in rows

Another approach, and one that has more potential for richness of design, is to work in

A square worked in rounds

rounds, from the centre outwards, increasing regularly at the four corners. As long as the increases are accurately calculated – they can be assessed by placing a mirror at an angle of 45 degrees across the pattern – this method should give a well-formed square, and any edging is an extension of the square already in progress rather than a separate addition.

CIRCULAR SHAWLS

These are worked from the centre outwards, and increases need to be carefully planned and meticulously executed to prevent fluting or other distortion. Wheel designs, which are divided by spoke increases, are often most satisfactory, as the increases are then in obvious vertical alignment. An alluring whirlpool effect can be achieved if each increase is placed to the side of the increase beneath, rather than directly above, it.

A wheel design worked in rounds and, right, a whirlpool design worked in rounds

TRIANGULAR SHAWLS

The simplest triangular shawls (also called half-shawls) relate to the diamond-shaped square. They can be worked in rows from a point, with increases made at each side until the full measurement is attained, or they can

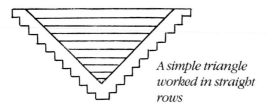

A simple triangle worked in straight rows

be started at the full measure and decreases worked at both sides until the point is reached. Whichever method is chosen, any edging is added to the two short sides only, although the long shoulder edge often needs reinforcing so that it can withstand the extra strain to which it is subjected.

An alternative and more satisfactory way of forming a triangular shawl is based on the square worked with corner increases. Work begins at the centre of the shoulder edge and proceeds in rows, keeping a full corner increase in the middle of each row, and a half-corner increase at the ends. As with a full square, any edging is an extension of the work already in progress.

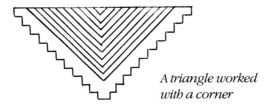

A triangle worked with a corner

Victorian women wore a bewildering variety of shawl shapes, some of which are more properly described as capes, as they often incorporated a hood, which would be drawn around the face with ribbons.

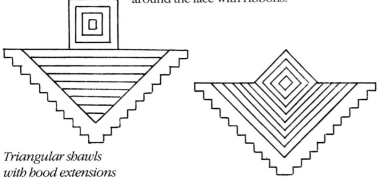

Triangular shawls with hood extensions

EDGINGS

Edgings are usually worked lengthways, directly on to the main body of the shawl, and crochet gives excellent results when this method is used. However, there was a short-lived Edwardian fashion for working a separate edging, widthways, and attaching it afterwards. There seems little reason for this unnecessary fad, and it was probably no more than an attempt to copy the contemporary knitted shawls on which edgings were worked widthways.

When working the first row or round of a crochet edging, the layout of pattern repeats will not necessarily coincide with the layout of pattern on the main body, or ground, of the shawl. These days we are accustomed to have every stitch accounted for, but in the past a worker would happily ease and adjust her spacing as necessary. The old method was freer, and it should be adopted with the designs described here wherever stitch counts are not exactly compatible.

FURTHER CONSIDERATIONS

Reversibility is important in a shawl, for both sides are on view. Strictly speaking, crochet that is worked in rounds has a right and wrong side, although in practice the difference is usually slight and is hardly worth considering in the context of the design as a whole. Nevertheless, nineteenth-century shawl-makers sometimes meticulously reversed their direction of work after each round in order to allow for this difference.

The centre, or ground, of a shawl is usually worked in a comparatively small, neat pattern that is devoid of long chains and excessively open structures. Such patterns are sometimes described as 'everlasting', and indeed the continual repeats can seem to go on for ever. Plain trebles or half-trebles, when loosely worked, will stretch on dressing to form a more attractive ground than might be expected. Indeed, half-trebles were once known as maud stitch, maud being an old Scottish name for a plaid or shawl.

YARN REQUIREMENTS

'The quantity of wool required will, of course, depend on the size the shawl is intended to be,' announced *Weldon's Practical Crochet,* somewhat impractically, in 1889. If supplies ran short, the maker either accepted a small shawl, or, as was more common, worked a few rounds of contrasting colour into the border.

If exact size is important, the only way to estimate quantities accurately for a particular combination of yarn, pattern and tension is to work a known amount of yarn and so calculate personal requirements. So much depends, not only on individual workmanship, but on the density of the pattern or patterns chosen, but, as a general guide, for a shawl approximately 48in (122cm) square, measured after dressing, allow:

5oz (150gm) of singles lace yarn
8oz (225gm) of 2-ply lace yarn
12oz (350gm) of standard 3-ply fingering
16oz (450gm) of standard 4-ply fingering

Similar quantities can be allowed for a circular shawl, but a triangular half-shawl needs more than half the quantities suggested – for example, allow 10oz (300gm) of standard 4-ply. These weights apply to pure wool, but there is no reason why acrylic or other yarns should not be substituted and allowance made for their different densities.

Singles yarns (the term 1-ply is a misnomer, as the word ply infers more than one strand) and various 2-ply lace yarns are obtainable from specialist machine knitting and weaving suppliers. Such yarns are often lightly oiled preparatory to machine use, and they may need to be washed after the shawl is finished.

Shetland lace wool, a 2-ply, is the traditional choice for crochet shawls. It should not be confused with the more popular 2-ply Shetland 'jumper' weight, which is a sturdier wool altogether. There is also a Shetland lace wool called 'cobweb', which is a very fine singles yarn. Shetland wools are still sold in hanks. This can be useful if a fringe is to be added as the hank can be cut directly into the appropriate lengths.

Baby wools, which are softer than the Shetlands, are also obtainable in 2-ply lace weights, although bulk varies considerably with different spinners. (Patons is the finest 2-ply baby wool currently available.)

There are various systems of yarn measurement, or count, which enable a greater accuracy of sizing than the ply system with which the general handknitter or crochet-worker is familiar. The finest shawls in this collection were made from a singles wool of 75 tex, and some of the other shawls were made from a 2/16 worsted count (an 'average' 2-ply, which is very similar to Shetland lace wool). A comparison of counts is complicated, and is in any case of more concern to the machine knitter. For a full explanation, see the relevant books cited in the Bibliography.

TENSION

As stated with the pattern samples, tension should be loose, much looser in fact than would be considered correct when working a fitted garment, not only because such looseness will enhance a shawl's lacy qualities but because so many fibres have a tendency to mat with long use.

HOOK REQUIREMENTS

Details of the hooks used are given with each shawl design, the sizes most generally used being 4.00mm or 4.50mm (US sizes F and G). However, do not hesitate to make test samples with different sized hooks to discover which gives the most pleasing effect for a particular yarn. The precise size of a hook is not as important as the manner in which it is wielded and the fabric produced.

Victorian ladies were never unduly concerned with quantities or sizes, and many an old pattern began: 'Procure best quality Shetland wool and a rather coarse bone crochet needle.' (Hooks were frequently called needles in the nineteenth century.)

Old bone hooks can still be found at antique markets, and they are often more pleasant to use than mass-produced modern hooks. Badly stained bone will respond to drastic cleaning with kitchen scouring powder, which should then be well rinsed off, and the bone should be dried immediately. A serviceable crochet hook needs to be smoothly polished, with a well-pointed head that can be easily pushed through the stitches, and a well-defined notch to catch the yarn. Sometimes it is possible to improve the shape of a blunted or damaged bone hook by the judicious use of a nail file and emery paper.

The size of an old hook can be determined with a knitting needle gauge. The shaft of a hook is measured, not the head, and if the hook in question has a shaft that gradually increases in size, the measurement should be made near the head, where the stitches will normally be worked.

DRESSING CROCHET LACE FABRICS

Dressing, or blocking, is essential if lace patterns are to be displayed at their best. The process stretches the work and opens up the whole structure, usually increasing the overall dimensions by at least a quarter.

The traditional way of dressing a shawl is to leave it rolled up in a wet towel, until its fibres are evenly moist. Spread a sheet over a carpeted floor in a room that will not be disturbed, lay the damp shawl on this, and stretch and pin the shawl evenly to an accurate shape. The fabric will always stretch more and require more pins, and the whole task will take longer to complete than one expects. Leave the shawl pinned into position until it is quite dry.

Pure wools retain their shape well after dressing, but will require redressing after each washing. Manmade fibres need an additional heat treatment to set their shape, but once set should need no further redressing. To set a shawl of manmade or mixed fibres, hold a steam iron over the stretched work so that the iron hovers above the surface, releasing steam but without exerting any pressure on the fabric. *Be very careful not to compress the fibres.*

'. . . and her shawl would not keep right, and now and then I drew it round her with my arm . . .'

David Copperfield, Charles Dickens, 1850

This method for shaping corners in a square shell shawl was published in *Mrs Leach's Fancy Work Basket* in 1889. However, the complete design with its leafy edging is from *The Children's Encyclopaedia*, edited by Arthur Mee and first published as a partwork in 1910.

The shawl illustrated was worked in 2-ply acrylic yarn using a 4.00mm hook. For a guide to yarn requirements see the section in Preliminary Planning. Set aside approximately one-third of the total yarn allowance for the edging.

Start at the centre with 6ch, ss to join into a ring.

1st round: 3ch, 15tr into ring, ss to top of 3ch to join.

2nd round: 3ch, 4tr between 3ch and 1st tr, *miss 4tr, 8tr between 4th and 5th tr. Repeat from * twice more, 3tr into same place as 4tr at beginning, ss to top of 3ch to join.

3rd round: 3ch, 2tr between 3ch and 1st tr, 4tr between 2nd and 3rd tr, *4tr between 2nd and 3rd tr of next group, 4tr between 4th and

5th, 4tr between 6th and 7th. Repeat from * twice more, 4tr between 2nd and 3rd tr of next group, 1tr into same place as 2tr at beginning, ss to top of 3ch to join.

4th round: 3ch, 4tr into centre of corner shell, *(4tr into centre of next shell) twice, 8tr into centre of corner shell. Repeat from * twice more, (4tr into centre of next shell) twice, 3tr into same place as 4tr at beginning, ss to join.

5th round: 3ch, 2tr into centre of corner group [i.e. between 2 corner shells], *(4tr into centre of next shell) 4 times, 4tr between 2 corner shells. Repeat from * twice more, (4tr into centre of next shell) 4 times, 1tr into same place as 2tr at beginning, ss to top of 3ch to join.

Repeat the 4th and 5th rounds with an increasing number of shells on each side, for the size required, ending with a 5th round.

Edging

This consists of three rounds of the *Shell and Bar* pattern (see page 15), followed by variations of the *Feather and Bar* (see page 60). It has sufficient fullness to spread round the corners without special shaping.

1st round: 1dc into centre of corner shell, 2ch, *4tr into centre of next shell, 2ch, 1dc into centre of following shell, 2ch. Repeat from * around the entire shawl, ending with 4tr into last shell, 2ch, 1dc into dc at beginning. **N.B.** 1dc should fall centrally on the 1st and 3rd corners, while a shell should fall on the 2nd and 4th corners.

Continue from the diagram, working the rounds in a continuous spiral – i.e., the dc that ends one round also begins the next. The base row of the diagram represents the 1st round, given above. For each picot of the outer edging work 4ch, ss to top of previous tr.

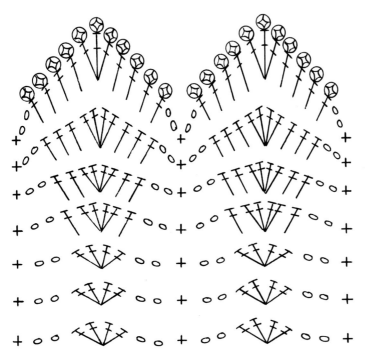

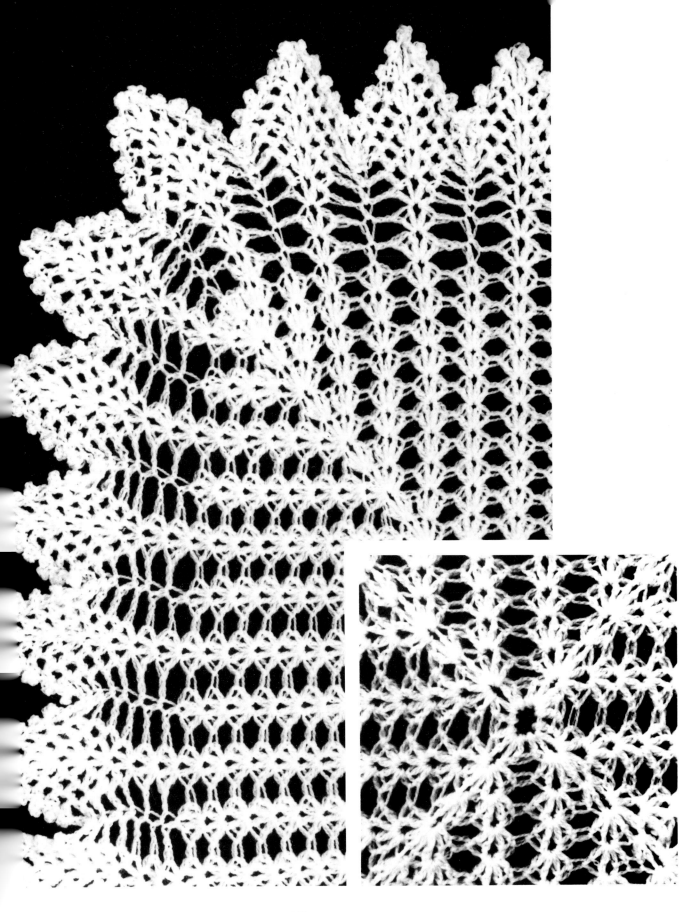

This design has the same shell centre as the previous *Shell and Leaf Shawl* but with a plainer version of the *Feather and Bar* edging (see page 60).

The shawl illustrated was worked in 2-ply baby wool using a 4.00mm hook. For a guide to yarn requirements see the section in Preliminary Planning. Set aside approximately one-quarter of the total yarn allowance for the edging.

Start at the centre and work a square in the basic shell pattern, as given for the *Shell and Leaf Shawl*, ending with a 4th round.

Edging

1st round: 1dc between 2 corner shells, *1ch, 1tr between 1st and 2nd tr of next shell, 4tr between 2nd and 3rd tr of same shell and 1tr between 3rd and 4th tr, 1ch, 1dc into centre of next shell. Repeat from *, working into every shell, and also working between the 2 shells at each corner. End with 1dc into dc at beginning. **N.B.** 1dc should fall centrally on the 1st and 3rd corners, while a feather should fall centrally on the 2nd and 4th corners.

Continue from the diagram, working the rounds in a continuous spiral – i.e., the dc that ends one round also begins the next. The base row of the diagram represents the 1st round, given above. There is no special shaping for the corners, but if they tend to pull, gradually increase the length of the corner chains.

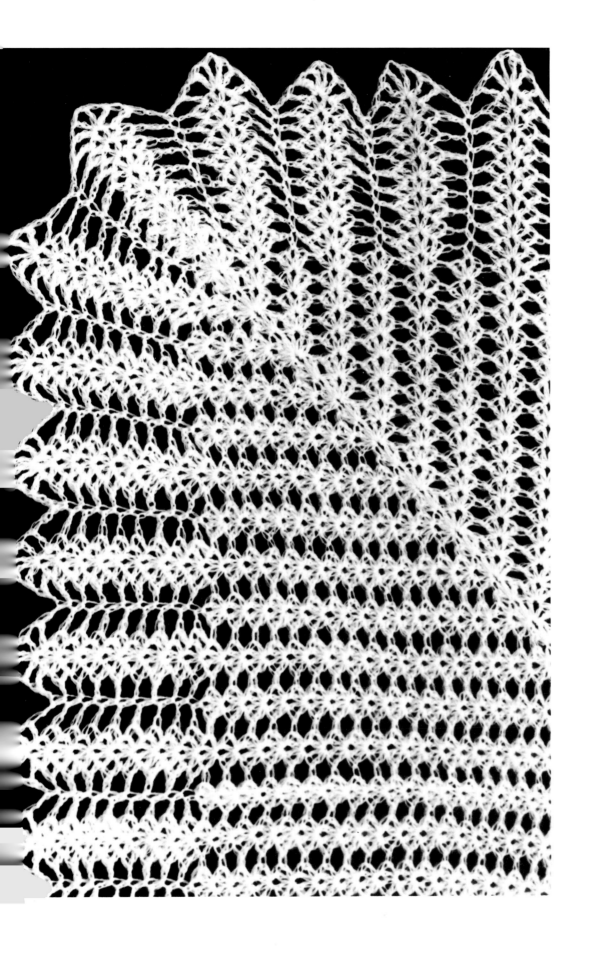

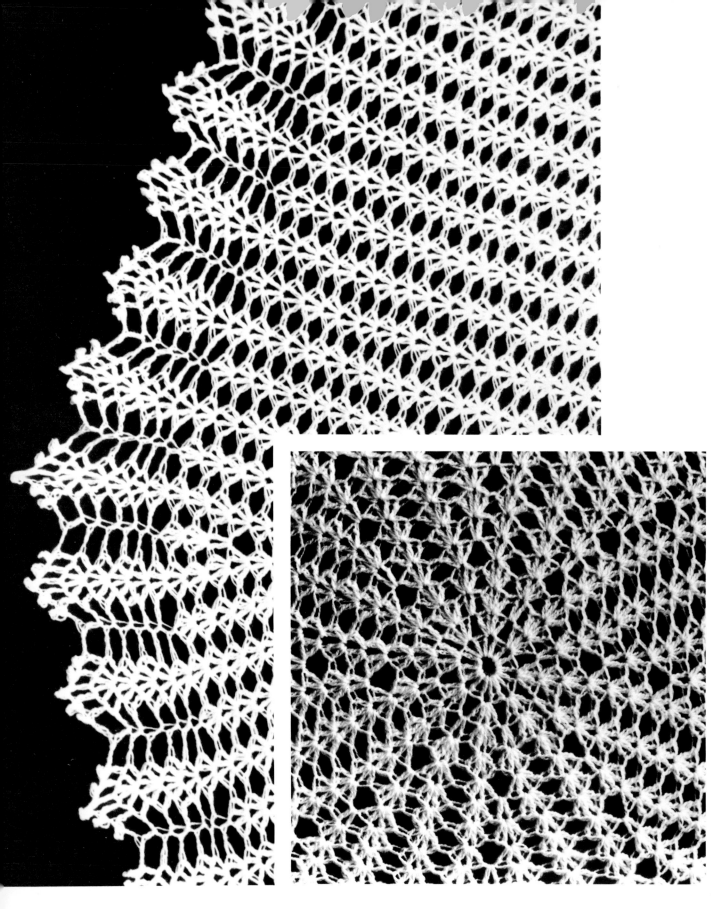

*T*he shape of this shawl is actually octagonal, but it will stretch into a circle when dressed. Its charm depends on the accuracy with which the increases, which radiate in curves to give a whirlpool effect, are worked.

The shawl illustrated was worked in 2-ply baby wool using a 4.00mm hook. For a guide to yarn requirements see the section in Preliminary Planning. Set aside approximately one-quarter of the total yarn allowance for the edging.

Start at the centre with 8ch, ss to join into a ring.

1st round: 3ch, 15tr into ring, ss to top of 3ch to join.

2nd round: 3ch, 2tr between 3ch and 1st tr of previous round, 4tr between 2nd and 3rd tr, 4tr between 4th and 5th, and between 6th and 7th, 8th and 9th, 10th and 11th, 12th and 13th, 14th and 15th, ending with 1tr into same place as 2tr at beginning, ss to top of 3ch to join.

3rd round: 3ch, 2tr into centre of 1st shell, (2tr into space between shells, 4tr into centre of next shell) 7 times, 2tr into next space, 1tr into same place as 2tr at beginning, ss to top of 3ch to join.

4th round: 3ch, 2tr into centre of 1st shell, (4tr into centre of 2tr, 4tr into centre of next shell) 7 times, 4tr into centre of 2tr, 1tr into same place as 2tr at beginning, ss to top of 3ch to join.

5th round: 3ch, 2tr into centre of 1st shell, *4tr into centre of next shell. Repeat from * all around, ending with 1tr into same place as 2tr at beginning, ss to top of 3ch to join.

6th round: 3ch, 2tr into centre of 1st shell, *2tr into space between shells (4tr into centre of next shell) twice. Repeat from * all around, ending as before.

7th round: 3ch, 2tr into centre of 1st shell, *4tr into centre of 2tr, (4tr into centre of next shell) twice. Repeat from * all around, ending as before.

8th round: as 5th round.

9th round: 3ch, 2tr into centre of 1st shell, *2tr into space between shells, (4tr into centre of next shell) 3 times. Repeat from * all around, ending as before.

Continue in this way, increasing in every third round, for the size required, and ending with an even number of shells in each panel.

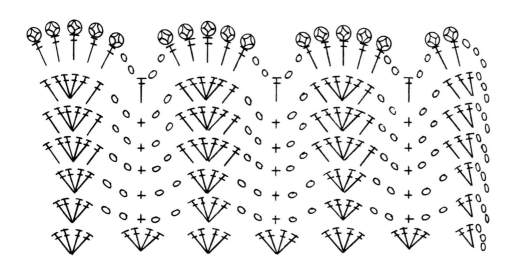

Edging

Continue from the diagram, ending each round in the usual way. The base row of the diagram represents the final round of the shawl centre. For each picot of the outer edge work 4ch, ss to top of previous tr.

This edging consists of two rounds of the *Shell and Bar* pattern (see page 15), followed by a variant of the *Feather and Bar* pattern (see page 60). Either can be extended in depth if required. If, as a result, the edging tends to pull, increase the number of chains or enlarge the feathers.

Variation

This shawl adapts well to a double-layered edging. Fold the original edging forward and insert the hook behind it into the last round of the shawl centre. Work an underlayer, making it a little deeper than the top layer. Due allowance should be made for the extra yarn.

*T*his square shawl in chain net needs to be made with a wiry yarn if it is to retain the shape of the chain stitches. Victorian patterns recommended 'ice' or 'eis' wool, which was a lace-weight mohair. When working the net, it is better to insert the hook into the chain rather than into the space made by the chain, as this too helps to retain the shape of the stitches.

The shawl illustrated was worked in 2-ply wool using a 4.00mm hook. For a guide to yarn requirements see the section in Preliminary Planning. However, since the net centre of this shawl is very open, it requires less yarn than recommended. Set aside a little more than one-third of the total yarn allowance for the edging.

Start at the centre with 8ch, ss to join into a ring.

1st round: (5ch, 1dc into next ch of ring) 7 times, 3ch, 1tr into ss.

2nd round: *5ch, 1dc into centre ch of next loop, (5ch, 1dc, 5ch, 1dc) into centre ch of following loop. Repeat from * twice more, 5ch, 1dc into centre ch of next loop, 5ch, ss to top of previous tr, 3ch, 1tr into top of same tr.

3rd round: *(5ch, 1dc into centre ch of next loop) twice, (5ch, 1dc, 5ch, 1dc) into centre ch of corner loop. Repeat from * twice more,

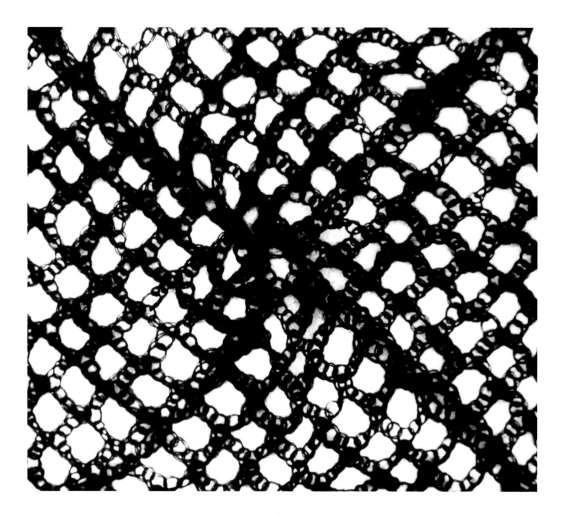

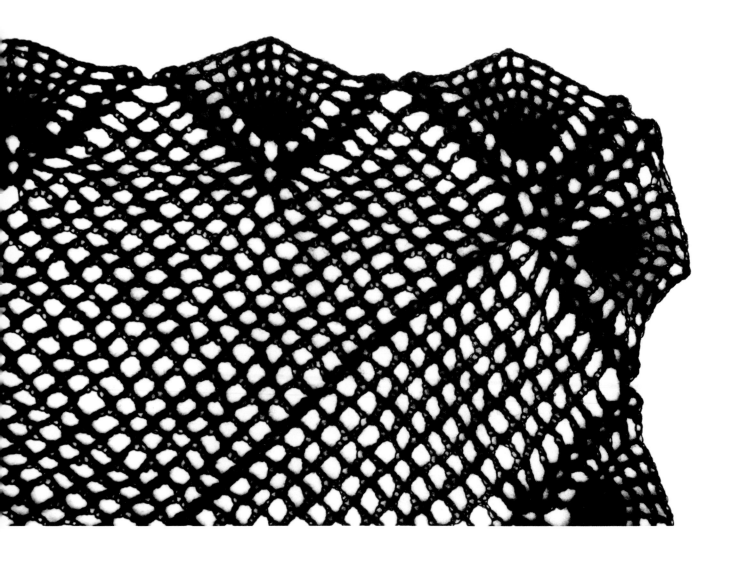

(5ch, 1dc into centre ch of next loop) twice, 5ch, ss to top of previous tr, 3ch, 1tr into top of same tr.

4th round: *(5ch, 1dc into centre ch of next loop) 3 times, (5ch, 1dc, 5ch, 1dc) into centre ch of corner loop. Repeat from * twice more, (5ch, 1dc into centre ch of next loop) 3 times, 5ch, ss to top of previous tr, 3ch, 1tr into top of same tr.

Continue in this way, gradually increasing the number of loops, for the size required, and ending with a number of loops on each side (including one corner loop) that is divisible by eight.

Edging

1st round: 5ch, 2tr into corner loop, *3ch, 1dc into centre ch of next 5ch loop, (5ch, 1dc into centre ch of next loop) 6 times, 3ch, (2tr, 2ch, 2tr) into next loop. Repeat from * all around, working (2tr, 2ch, 2tr, 2ch, 2tr) into each corner loop. Finish the round with (2tr, 2ch, 1tr) into first corner loop, ss to 3rd of 5ch at beginning.

Continue from the diagram, working the fan pattern twice at each corner, and ending each round with 1tr, ss to 3rd of 5ch. The base row of the diagram represents the 1st round, given above.

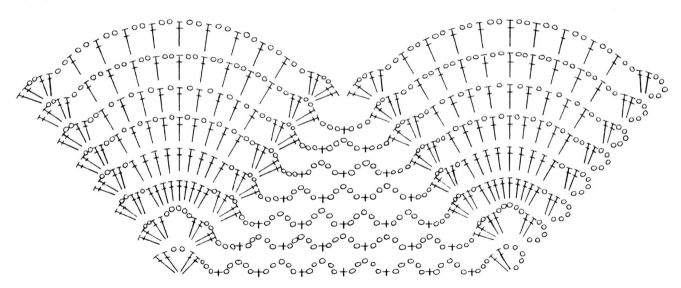

*T*his square design has a simple *Shell and Net* ground (see page 26), with a diamond-shaped border, which can be extended to any depth.

The shawl illustrated was worked in a 3-ply acrylic mixture using a 4.50mm hook. For a guide to yarn requirements see the section in Preliminary Planning. Set aside more than half the total yarn allowance for the deep border.

Start at the centre with 8ch, ss to join into a ring.

1st round: *5ch, miss 1ch of the ring, (1dc, 5ch, 1dc) into next ch. Repeat from * twice more, (5ch, miss 1ch, 1dc, 3ch, 1tr) into last ch.

2nd round: *5ch, 1dc into centre ch of next loop, (5ch, 1dc, 5ch, 1dc) into centre ch of following loop. Repeat from * twice more, 5ch, 1dc into centre ch of next loop, 5ch, 1dc into top of tr, 3ch, 1tr into top of same tr.

3rd round: *5ch, 1dc into centre ch of next loop, 5tr into next dc, 1dc into centre ch of following loop, (5ch, 1dc, 5ch, 1dc) into centre of corner loop. Repeat from * twice more, 5ch, 1dc into centre ch of next loop, 5tr into next dc, 1dc into centre ch of following loop, 5ch, 1dc into top of tr, 3ch, 1tr into top of same tr.

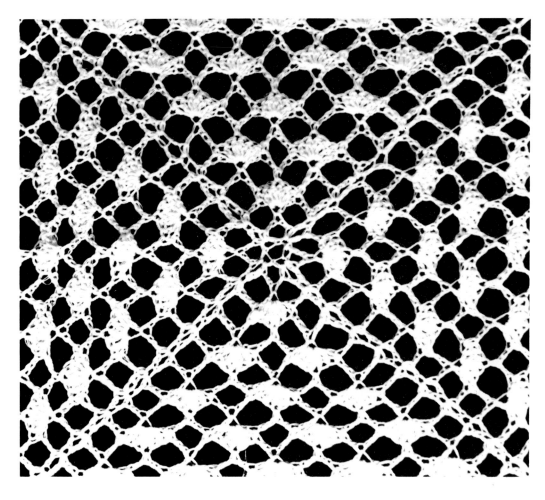

4th round: *5ch, 1dc into next loop, 5ch, 1dc into centre tr of shell, 5ch, 1dc into following loop, (5ch, 1dc, 5ch, 1dc) into corner loop. Repeat from * twice more, 5ch, 1dc into next loop, 5ch, 1dc into centre tr of shell, 5ch, 1dc into following loop, 5ch, 1dc into tr, 3ch, 1tr into tr.

5th round: *(5ch, 1dc into next loop, 5tr into next dc, 1dc into following loop) twice, (5ch, 1dc, 5ch, 1dc) into corner loop. Repeat from * twice more, (5ch, 1dc into next loop, 5tr into next dc, 1dc into following loop) twice, 5ch, 1dc into tr, 3ch, 1tr into tr.

6th round: *(5ch, 1dc into next loop, 5ch, 1dc into shell) twice, 5ch, 1dc into following loop, (5ch, 1dc, 5ch, 1dc) into corner loop. Repeat from * twice more, (5ch, 1dc into next loop, 5ch, 1dc into shell) twice, 5ch, 1dc into following loop, 5ch, 1dc into tr, 3ch, 1tr into tr.

7th round: As 5th round but with one extra shell on each side.

Continue in this way for the size required, ending with an odd number of shells on each side.

Border and edging

Continue from the diagram, ending each round in the usual way. The base row of the diagram represents the last round of the shawl centre, which is also the first round of the diamond border. Repeat from the 4th round for a depth of three diamonds (or as required) and finish with an edging to match the shawl centre.

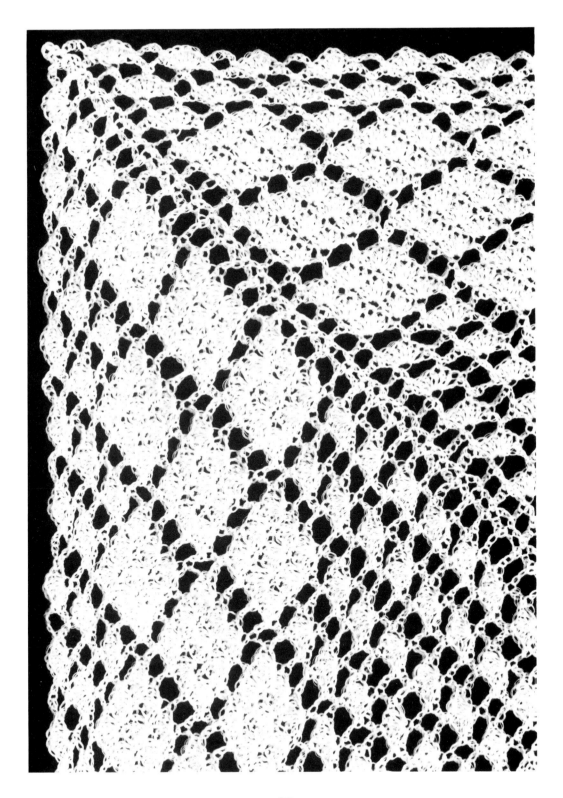

The *Cottage Shawl* is, of course, a larger version of the small patchwork square known today as the granny square that is generally used for blankets. The distinction between a heavy outdoor shawl and a crochet blanket is that traditionally a shawl was made in one piece, and a blanket, being much heavier, was made from an assembly of patches.

Treble-block designs with mitred corner increases were well established by the 1860s, and in 1862 Eléonore Riego, a famous Victorian needlewoman, gave this method for working a shawl corner in *La Mode Winter Book.*

When the square *Cottage Shawl* is worked in rounds, the join at the end of each round may be tackled in two ways. In one, the join falls in vertical alignment on one of the sides and is usually conspicuous. In the other, which is the version given below, the join falls at a corner mitre and is barely visible.

The shawl illustrated, with its Victorian bobble edging, was worked in 2-ply wool using a 4.00mm hook. For a guide to yarn requirements see the section in Preliminary Planning. Set aside a little less than one-quarter of the total yarn allowance for the bobble edging.

Start at the centre with 6ch, ss to join into a ring.
1st round: 5ch, (3tr into ring, 2ch) 3 times, 2tr into ring, ss to 3rd of 5ch to join.
2nd round: ss into space formed by 5ch, 5ch, 3tr into same space, 2ch *(3tr, 2ch, 3tr) into next 2ch space, 2ch. Repeat from * twice more, 2tr into same space as ss at beginning, ss to 3rd of 5ch to join.

3rd round: ss into space formed by 5ch, 5ch, 3tr into same space, *2ch, 3tr into next 2ch space, 2ch, (3tr, 2ch, 3tr) into next corner space. Repeat from * twice more, 2ch, 3tr into next space, 2ch, 2tr into same space as ss at beginning, ss to 3rd of 5ch to join.
4th round: ss into space formed by 5ch, 5ch, 3tr into same space, *(2ch, 3tr into next 2ch space) twice, 2ch, (3tr, 2ch, 3tr) into next corner space. Repeat from * twice more, (2ch, 3tr into next space) twice, 2ch, 2tr into same space as ss at beginning, ss to 3rd of 5ch to join.
Continue in this way, working an extra block into each side on all following rounds, for the size required.

Bobble edging

Work 1dc into corner space, *5ch, 10tr all into 3rd ch from hook, ss to top of first tr to form a cup-shaped bobble, 1ch, 1dc into next space on side of shawl. Repeat from * all around, working an extra bobble into each corner space.

Variations

1. Contrasting coloured borders make a more interesting design. To change colours, finish one with the final slipstitch of a round, and begin another with the first slipstitch of the following round.
2. The spaces between each block can be reduced by working 1ch instead of 2ch, or they can be enlarged to 3ch. The latter version was given for a shawl by S.F.A. Caulfeild and B.C. Saward in their *Dictionary of Needlework,* which was first published in 1882.
3. A fringe can replace the bobble edging.

'At 5.30 am I was awoke by the tramp of the factory girls . . . all in clog-shoon and most of them with shawls over their heads, all tramping to work in groups of two and three, and talking broad Lancashire audibly.'

from the diaries of Arthur Munby, 1873, *Victorian Working Women: Portraits from Life,* Michael Hiley (Gordon Fraser, 1979)

*T*his triangular design for a shoulder shawl is based on a version from *The Lady's Crochet Book* by 'E.M.C.', which was published in 1874. It is exactly half of the square *Cottage Shawl*, and it is characterized by the mitred corner increase, which falls at the centre back in wear.

The shawl illustrated was worked in 2 ply wool using a 4.00mm hook. For a guide to yarn requirements see the section in Preliminary Planning. Set aside between one-eighth and one-sixth of the total yarn allowance for the fringe.

Start at the centre shoulder line with 6ch, ss to join into a ring.
1st row: 3ch, 3tr into ring, 1ch, 4tr into ring, 3ch, turn.
2nd row: 3tr between 1st and 2nd tr, 1ch, (3tr, 1ch, 3tr) into next 1ch space, 1ch, 4tr at end between last tr and turning ch, 3ch, turn.
3rd row: 3tr between 1st and 2nd tr, 1ch, 3tr into next 1ch space, 1ch, (3tr, 1ch, 3tr) into centre 1ch space, 1ch, 3tr into following 1ch space, 1ch, 4tr at end between last tr and turning ch, 3ch, turn.
4th row: 3tr between 1st and 2nd tr, (1ch, 3tr into next space) twice, 1ch, (3tr, 1ch, 3tr) into centre space, (1ch, 3tr into next space) twice,

1ch, 4tr at end between last tr and turning ch, 3ch, turn.
Continue in this way, working an extra block on each side of the triangle on every row, for the size required.

The fringe
Unless the yarn is in a hank (when it can be cut directly), wind it round an appropriately sized card or book to yield cut lengths of approximately 12in (30cm) or as required, bearing in mind that there will be some contraction and take up when the yarn is attached. Use a hook to attach a trial piece first, to assess the number of strands that will look best and give an adequate knot – usually 4 lengths of yarn, which, when doubled, yield an 8-strand fringe. Distribute the fringes in alternate positions, and fill in the missing places afterwards in case the distribution or number of strands needs to be re-assessed. Unwanted kinks or curls in the yarn can be eliminated by dipping the fringe in warm water. As a finishing touch, trim the ends with scissors.

Variations
See the bobble edging and also the variations given for the square *Cottage Shawl* (page 88).

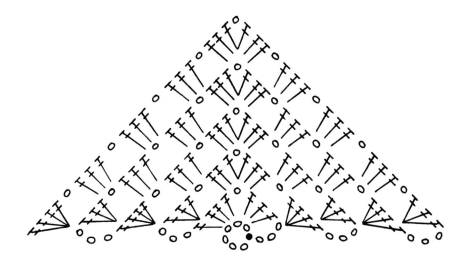

'So I left the washing up
and put on my bonnet
and shawl and went with
him . . .'

*Diaries of Hannah
Cullwick, Victorian
Maidservant,* 1863
(Virago Press, 1984)

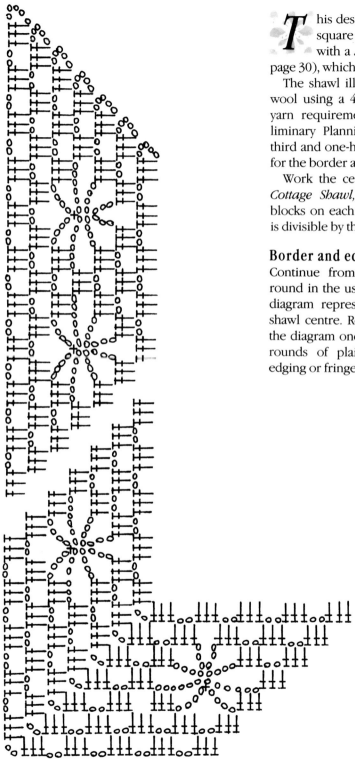

*T*his design has the same centre as the square *Cottage Shawl* (see page 88) with a *Spider and Block* border (see page 30), which can be extended as required.

The shawl illustrated was worked in 2-ply wool using a 4.00mm hook. For a guide to yarn requirements see the section in Preliminary Planning. Set aside between one-third and one-half of the total yarn allowance for the border and edging.

Work the centre as given for the square *Cottage Shawl,* ending with a number of blocks on each side (including corners) that is divisible by three.

Border and edging

Continue from the diagram, ending each round in the usual way. The base row of the diagram represents the final round of the shawl centre. Repeat from the 2nd round of the diagram once more, then finish with two rounds of plain treble blocks. A bobble edging or fringe can be added.

One advantage of this design is that it can be adapted easily to form a poncho by leaving a diagonal slit across the centre as a neck opening.

The shawl illustrated was worked in 4-ply acrylic yarn using a 6.00mm hook. For a guide to yarn requirements see the section in Preliminary Planning. Set aside approximately one-quarter of the total yarn allowance for the fringe.

Start with 7ch, 3tr into 7th ch from hook, 6ch, turn.

1st row: 3tr inserting the hook under the turning chain just made, 2ch, 3tr into loop made by foundation chain, 6ch, turn.

2nd row: 3tr under the turning chain, 2ch, 3tr into 2ch space, 2ch, 3tr into loop at end, 6ch, turn.

3rd row: 3tr under the turning chain, (2ch, 3tr into next 2ch space) twice, 2ch, 3tr into loop at end, 6ch, turn.

4th row: 3tr under the turning chain, (2ch, 3tr into next 2ch space) 3 times, 2ch, 3tr into loop at end, 6ch, turn.

Continue in this way until half the yarn allowance for the main shawl has been used. End with 3ch to turn, instead of the usual 6ch, in order to begin decreasing.

1st decrease row: 3tr into first 2ch space, *2ch, 3tr into next 2ch space. Repeat from *, ending with 3tr into 6ch loop, 3ch, turn.

2nd decrease row: 3tr into first 2ch space, *2ch, 3tr into next 2ch space. Repeat from * to end of row, 3ch, turn.

Repeat the 2nd decrease row till one block remains and the square is complete.

To make the fringe, see No. 7, *Cottage Shawl,* triangular version, (page 90).

Variation

To adapt the design for a poncho, work half the shawl as described. At the centre of the last row, mark the position for the neck opening of 12in (30cm) or the length required. Begin the 1st decrease row and work to the position marked for the opening, ending with a treble block. Work a length of chain stitches equal in number to the number of stitches to be missed, work a block into the next 2ch space after the opening and continue the row as set. In the following row, work blocks and spaces across the new foundation chain, making sure that the numbers correspond to the stitches missed.

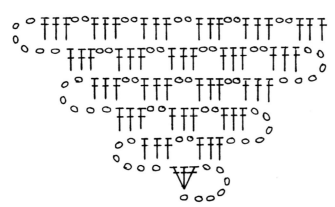

This circular design has a plain treble ground with radiating spoke increases and an edging of *Old Shale* (see page 52).

The shawl illustrated was worked in 2-ply wool using a 4.50mm hook. For a guide to yarn requirements see the section in Preliminary Planning. Set aside between one-quarter and one-third of the total yarn allowance for the edging.

Start at the centre with 8ch, ss to join into a ring.

1st round: 3ch, 23tr into the ring, ss to top of 3ch.

2nd round: 3ch, (2tr into next tr, 1tr into following tr) 11 times, 2tr into next tr, ss to top of 3ch.

3rd round: 3ch, 1tr into next tr, *2tr into following tr, 1tr into each of next 2tr. Repeat from * 10 times more, 2tr into following tr, ss to top of 3ch.

4th round: 3ch, 1tr into each of next 2tr, *2tr into following tr, 1tr into each of next 3tr. Repeat from * 10 times more, 2tr into following tr, ss to top of 3ch.

5th round: 3ch, 1tr into each of next 3tr, *2tr

into following tr, 1tr into each of next 4tr. Repeat from * 10 times more, 2tr into following tr, ss to top of 3ch.

Continue in this way, increasing 12 times in every round, for the size required. In order to accommodate the edging, the total number of trebles in the final round should be divisible by 11. However, if this is inconvenient, the first round of the edging can be adjusted to fit by occasionally working two trebles into one stitch.

Edging

Continue from the diagram, ending each round with ss. The base row of the diagram represents the final round of the shawl centre. Repeat the last round of edging 3 times more for the shawl illustrated.

The depth of this edging can be extended. If, as a result, it tends to pull, either change to a larger hook or enlarge the 2ch spaces to 3ch.

Variation

A few rounds of the edging can be worked in a contrasting colour to accentuate the waves of *Old Shale.*

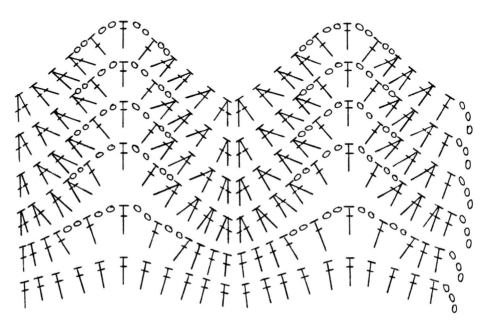

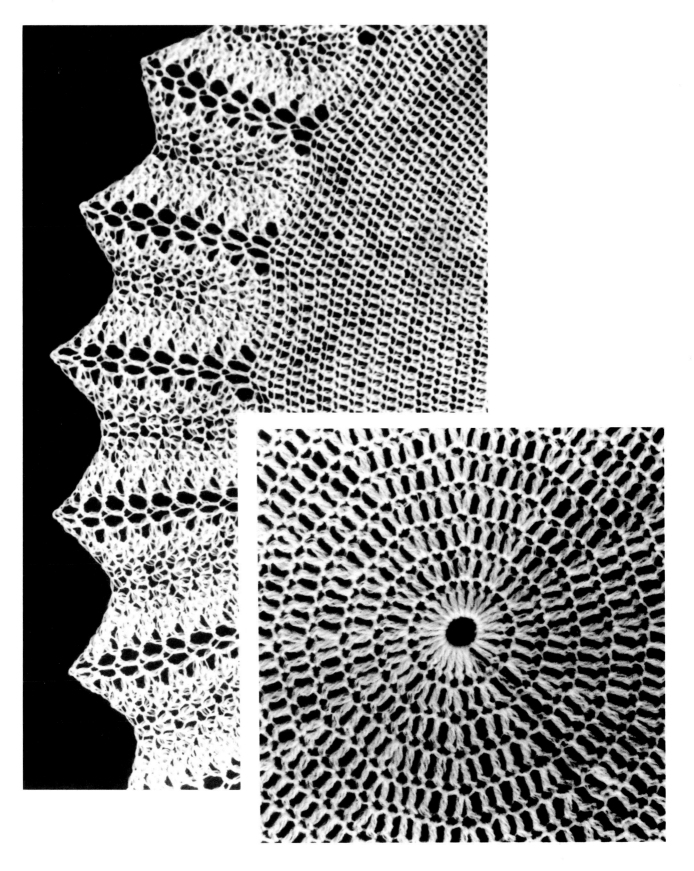

'Swaddling sounds old fashioned, but it can make the small, fretful baby feel more comfortable and secure. Fold a blanket or shawl in a triangle and lie the baby on it. Fold one corner over the baby and tuck it firmly under him. Do the same with the other corner, then tuck the point of the shawl under the baby's feet.'

You and Your Baby: The First Twelve Months (Dorling Kindersley Ltd in conjunction with the British Medical Association, 1987)

*T*his square design has a plain treble ground edged with a variant of *Waves* (see page 50).

The shawl illustrated was worked in singles wool, 75 tex, using a 3.50mm hook for the ground and a 4.00mm hook for the edging. For a guide to yarn requirements see the section in Preliminary Planning. Set aside approximately one-third of the total allowance for the edging.

Start at the centre with 6ch, ss to join into a ring.

1st round: 3ch, 15tr into the ring, ss to top of 3ch.

2nd round: 3ch, 2tr into next tr, (1tr into each of next 3tr, 4tr into following tr) 3 times, 1tr into each of next 3tr, 1tr into same place as 2tr at beginning, ss to top of 3ch.

3rd round: 3ch, 2tr into next tr, (1tr into each of next 6tr, 4tr into following tr) 3 times, 1tr into each of next 6tr, 1tr into same place as 2tr at beginning, ss to top of 3ch.

4th round: 3ch, 2tr into next tr, (1tr into each of next 9tr, 4tr into following tr) 3 times, 1tr into each of next 9tr, 1tr into same place as 2tr at beginning, ss to top of 3ch.

Continue in this way for the size required. In order to accommodate the edging, the total number of trebles on each side (including the

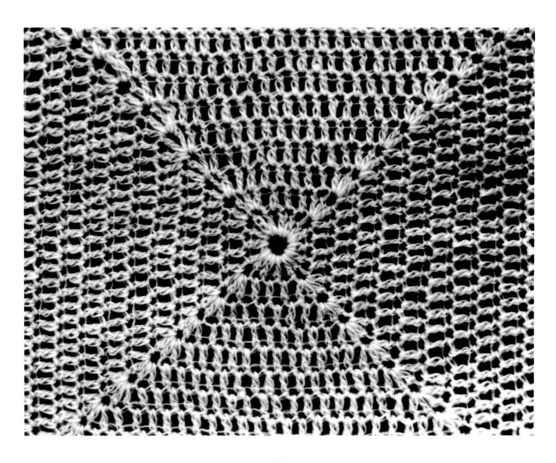

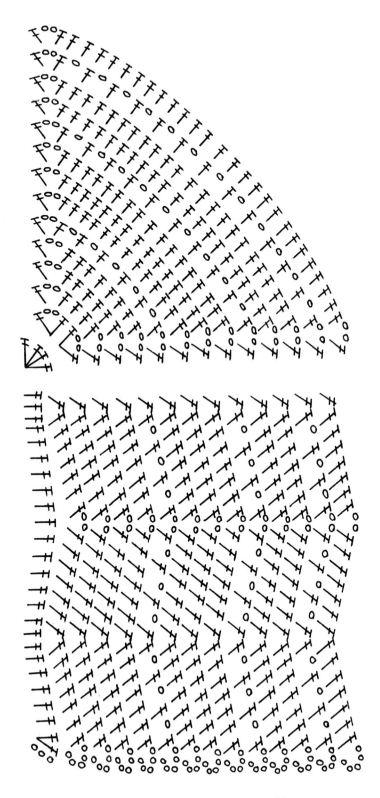

increases) should be divisible by 15, plus one extra. However, if this is inconvenient, the first round of waves can be adjusted to fit by missing only one treble instead of two when forming the spaces.

Edging
Change to the larger hook and continue from the diagram, ending each round with ss. The base row of the diagram represents the final round of the shawl centre.

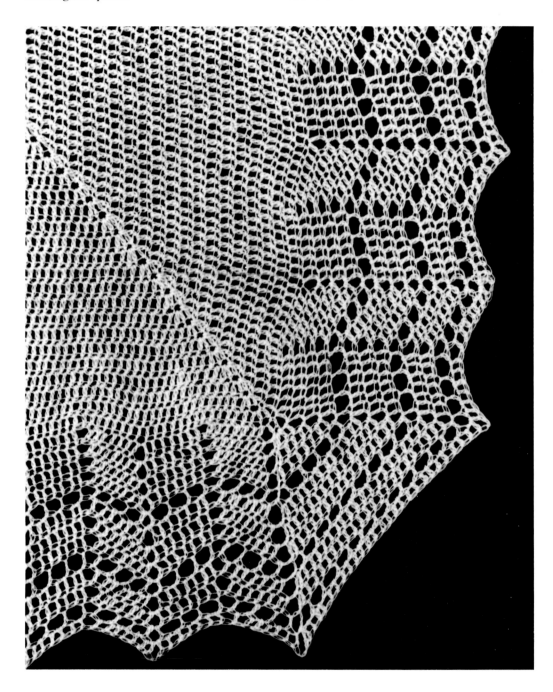

*P*lain trebles worked in diagonal rows form the ground of this shawl. The edging was published in *Weldon's Practical Crochet,* 5th series, 1887, and it may have been given its unusual name, *Willow* *Pattern,* because the puff stitches were thought to resemble the catkins of the pussy willow.

The shawl illustrated was worked in 2/16 worsted using a 4.50mm hook. For a guide to

yarn requirements see the section in Preliminary Planning. However, this design requires more yarn than usual because the puffs take extra. Set aside almost half of the total yarn allowance for the edging.

Start with 7ch.
1st row: 3tr into 7th ch from hook, 6ch, turn.
2nd row: (1tr into next tr) 3 times, 3tr into loop at end, 6ch, turn.
3rd row: (1tr into next tr) 6 times, 3tr into loop at end, 6ch, turn.
4th row: (1tr into next tr) 9 times, 3tr into loop at end, 6ch, turn.
Continue in this way until approximately half the yarn allowance for the centre has been used. There should be an equal, and even, number of loops on each side. End the last row with 4ch instead of the usual 6ch, ready to begin decreasing.
Decrease row: miss 3tr, *1tr into next tr. Repeat from * to end of row, 4ch, turn.
Repeat the decrease row until 3tr remain.

Turn with 4ch, miss 2tr, 1tr into 3rd tr in order to form a final corner loop. Do not break the yarn. There should be an even number of loops around the entire edge of the shawl.

Edging
See the *Feather and Puff* sample (page 62) for directions for working the puff stitches.

1st round: 7tr into next loop along side, *(1 puff, 2ch, 1 puff) into next loop, 8tr into following loop. Repeat from * all round, working (1 puff, 2ch, 1 puff, 2ch, 1 puff, 2ch, 1 puff) into the four corner loops. Do not finish this round, or any of the following rounds, by joining with ss.
Continue from the diagram, working the rounds in a continuous spiral. The base row of the diagram represents the 1st round, given above. For each picot on the outer edge work 4ch, ss to top of previous tr.

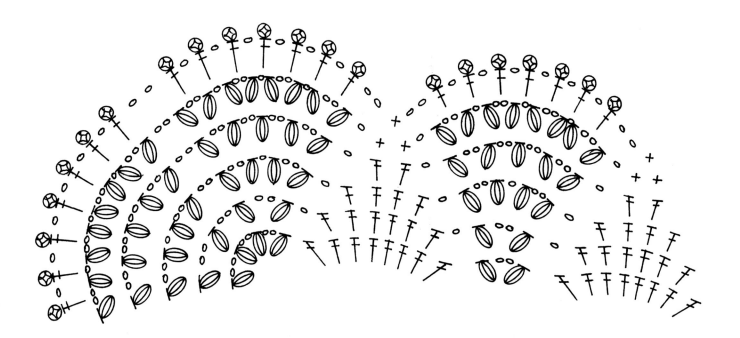

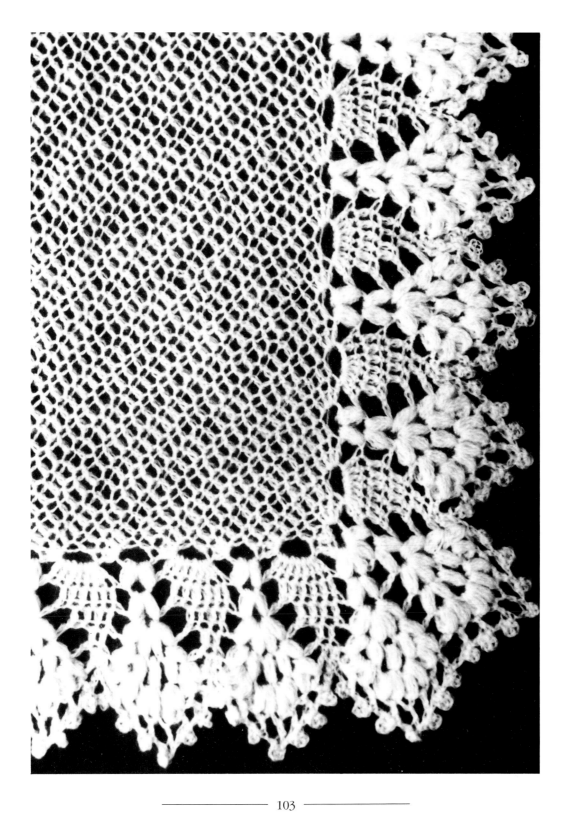

*T*his design has the same square centre as the *Willow Pattern Shawl* (see page 101) and is edged with *Double Fan and Shell* (see page 42).

The shawl illustrated was worked in 2-ply wool using a 4.50mm hook for the treble ground and a 4.00mm hook for the edging. For a guide to yarn requirements see the section in Preliminary Planning. Set aside approximately one-third of the total yarn allowance for the edging.

Work the centre as given for the *Willow Pattern Shawl,* similarly, working a final loop without breaking the yarn. There should be an even number of loops around the edge.

Edging

Change to the smaller hook.

1st round: 4ch, turn, 8dtr into final corner loop, *(2tr, 2ch, 2tr) into next loop around edge, 8dtr into following loop. Repeat from * all round, working 16dtr into the corner loops, and ending with 7dtr, ss to top of 4ch in order to complete the first corner.

Continue from the diagram, finishing each round with ss. The base row of the diagram represents the 1st round, given above. Repeat the 3rd and 4th rounds twice more, or for the depth required, before working the final round.

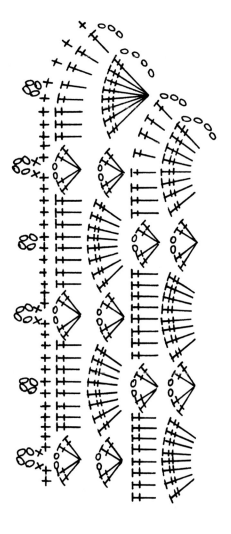

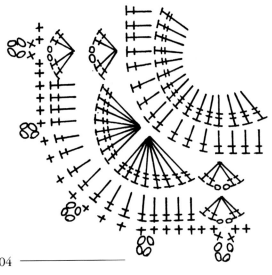

This design was published by *Needle-craft* of Manchester, *c.*1906. It was then reproduced by J. & J. Baldwin of Halifax, Yorkshire, in its early editions of *Woolcraft,* from which so many women learnt to crochet in the 1920s and 1930s, and which, no doubt, accounts for its success as a perennial classic. It was especially popular as a tennis shawl in the 1930s.

The shawl is worked in treble net with a *Feather and Puff* border (see page 62), and although it actually has seven sides, it will stretch into a circle when dressed.

The shawl illustrated was worked in 2-ply wool using a 4.50mm hook. For a guide to yarn requirements see the section in Preliminary Planning. Set aside approximately one-third of the total yarn allowance for the edging.

Start at the centre with 6ch, ss to join into a ring.

1st round: 4ch, (1tr into ring, 1ch) 6 times, ss to 3rd of 4ch to join.

2nd round: 4ch, 1tr into 1st space, 1ch, *(1tr, 1ch, 1tr) into next space, 1ch. Repeat from * 5 times more, ss to 3rd of 4ch.

3rd round: 4ch, 1tr into next space, 1ch, *1tr into next space, 1ch, (1tr, 1ch, 1tr) into following space, 1ch. Repeat from * 5 times more, 1tr into next space, 1ch, ss to 3rd of 4ch.

4th round: 3ch, yarn-over-hook, insert hook into next space, draw yarn through and pull up to the height of a tr, (yarn-over-hook, insert hook into same space and draw yarn through and up as before) twice, yarn-over-hook and draw through all loops to complete the puff, 2ch, 1 puff into same space, *1ch, (1tr

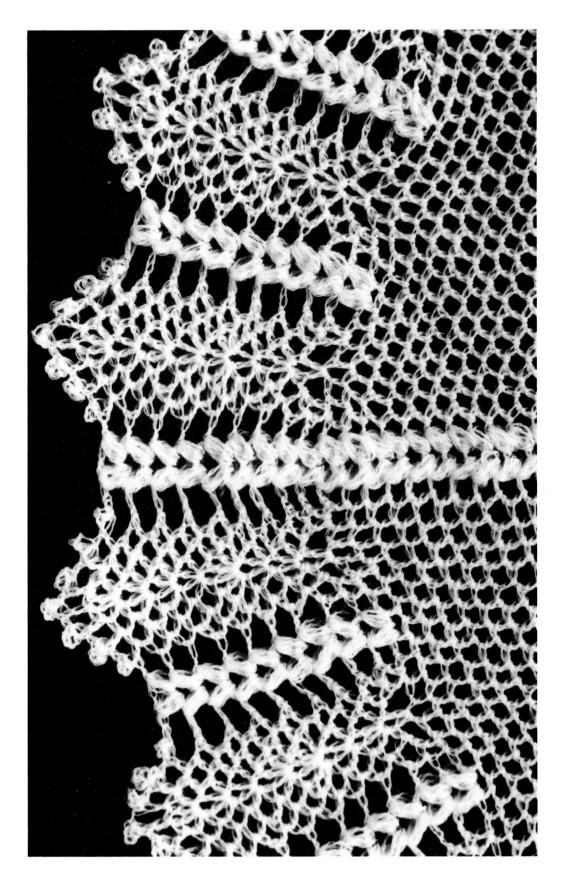

into next space, 1ch) twice, (1 puff, 2ch, 1 puff) into following space. Repeat from * 5 times more, 1ch, (1tr into next space, 1ch) twice, ss to top of 1st puff.

5th round: ss into space between puffs, 3ch, *(1 puff, 2ch, 1 puff) into space between puffs, 1ch, (1tr into next space, 1ch) 3 times. Repeat from * 6 times more, ss to top of 1st puff.

6th round: ss into space between puffs, 3ch, *(1 puff, 2ch, 1 puff) into space between puffs, 1ch, (1tr into next space, 1ch) 4 times. Repeat from * 6 times more, ss to top of 1st puff.

Continue in this way, working 1tr extra on each side in successive rounds, for the size required. In order to accommodate the edging, the total number of spaces on each side (including one space between puffs) should be divisible by eight.

Edging

Continue from the diagram, ending each round in the usual way. The base row of the diagram represents the final round of the shawl centre. For each picot on the outer edge work 4ch, ss to top of previous tr.

This *Feather and Puff* edging can be made deeper and the feathers increased in size if required.

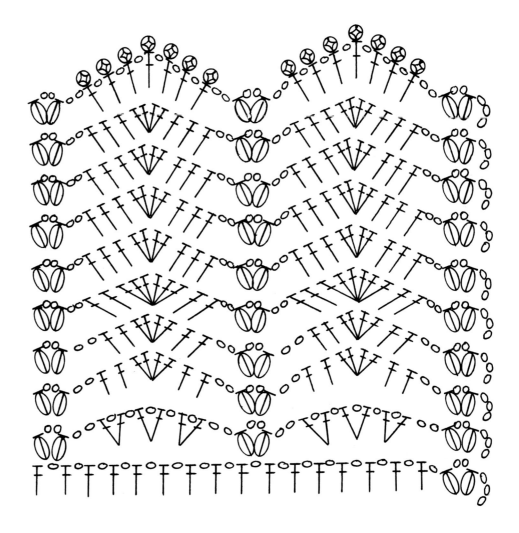

*T*reble net is used for the ground of this design. The shawl illustrated was worked in 2-ply wool using a 4.50mm hook. For a guide to yarn requirements see the section in Preliminary Planning. Set aside approximately one-quarter of the total yarn allowance for the edging.

Start at the centre shoulder line with 4ch, join into a ring with ss.

1st row: 4ch, (1tr, 2ch, 1tr, 1ch, 1tr) into ring, turn.

2nd row: 4ch, 1tr into 1st space, 1ch, (3tr, 1ch, 3tr) into 2ch space, 1ch, (3tr, 1ch, 1tr) into last space, turn.

3rd row: 4ch, 1tr into 1st space, 1ch, 1tr into 2nd tr of group, 1ch, 1tr into next space, 1ch, 1tr into 2nd tr of group, 1ch, (1tr, 1ch, 1tr) into next space, 1ch, 1tr into 2nd tr of next group, 1ch, 1tr into next space, 1ch, (3tr, 1ch, 1tr) into last space, turn.

4th row: 4ch, 1tr into 1st space, 1ch, 1tr into 2nd tr of group, 1ch, (1tr into next space, 1ch) 3 times, (3tr, 1ch, 3tr) into centre space, 1ch, (1tr into next space, 1ch) 4 times, (3tr, 1ch, 1tr) into last space, turn.

5th row: 4ch, 1tr into 1st space, 1ch, 1tr into 2nd tr of group, 1ch, (1tr into next space, 1ch) 5 times, 1tr into 2nd tr of group, 1ch, (1tr, 1ch, 1tr) into centre space, 1ch, 1tr into 2nd tr of next group, 1ch, (1tr into next space, 1ch) 5 times, (3tr, 1ch, 1tr) into last space, turn.

6th row: 4ch, 1tr into 1st space, 1ch, 1tr into 2nd tr of group, 1ch, (1tr into next space, 1ch) 7 times, (3tr, 1ch, 3tr) into centre space, 1ch, (1tr into next space, 1ch) 8 times, (3tr, 1ch, 1tr) into last space, turn.

7th row: 4ch, 1tr into 1st space, 1ch, 1tr into

'. . . a triangular shawl, its corners draggling on the stubble . . .'

Tess of the D'Urbervilles, Thomas Hardy, 1891

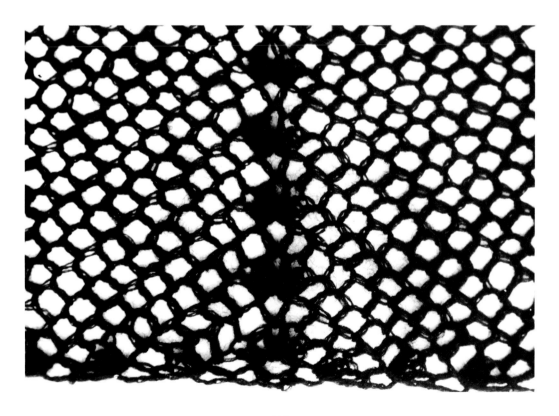

2nd tr of group, 1ch, (1tr into next space, 1ch) 9 times, 1tr into 2nd tr of group, 1ch, (1tr, 1ch, 1tr) into centre space, 1ch, 1tr into 2nd tr of next group, 1ch, (1tr into next space, 1ch) 9 times, (3tr, 1ch, 1tr) into last space, turn.

Continue in this way for the size required, ending with a row like the 7th.

Edging

Continue in rows from the diagram, turning each row with 4ch. The base row of the diagram represents the final row of treble net. At the corner, work a fan of 10dtr instead of the usual 7dtr. If necessary, adjust the layout of the pattern by missing fewer 1ch spaces before and after the corner fan. For each picot work 4ch, ss to top of previous dtr.

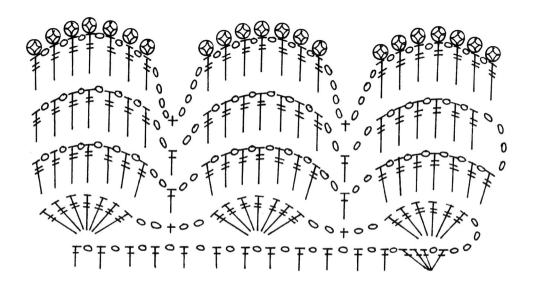

his design was published by *Needle-craft* of Manchester, *c.*1906. The ground is worked in *Shells and Triangles* (see page 17), with an inner border of puff stitches and a variant of *Shell and Bar* (see page 15) as an outer edging.

The shawl illustrated was worked in 2/16 worsted using a 4.50mm hook. For a guide to yarn requirements see the section in Pre-liminary Planning. However, this design requires more yarn than usual because the puffs take extra. Set aside approximately two-thirds of the total yarn allowance for the puff border and outer edging.

Start at the centre with 5ch, ss to join into a ring.

1st round: 4ch, (1tr into ring, 1ch) 7 times, ss to 3rd of 4ch at beginning.

2nd round: ss into 1ch space, 6ch, 1tr into same space, *(1tr, 3ch, 1tr) into next space to make a triangle. Repeat from * 6 times more, ss to 3rd of 6ch.

3rd round: ss into next space, 6ch, 4tr into same space, *4tr into next triangle, (4tr, 3ch, 4tr) into following triangle. Repeat from * twice more, 4tr into next triangle, 3tr into first space, ss to 3rd of 6ch.

4th round: ss into corner space, 6ch, (1tr, 3ch, 1tr) into same space, *(1tr, 3ch, 1tr) between 2nd and 3rd tr of each of next 3 shells, (1tr, 3ch, 1tr, 3ch, 1tr, 3ch, 1tr) into corner space. Repeat from * twice more, (1tr, 3ch, 1tr) into

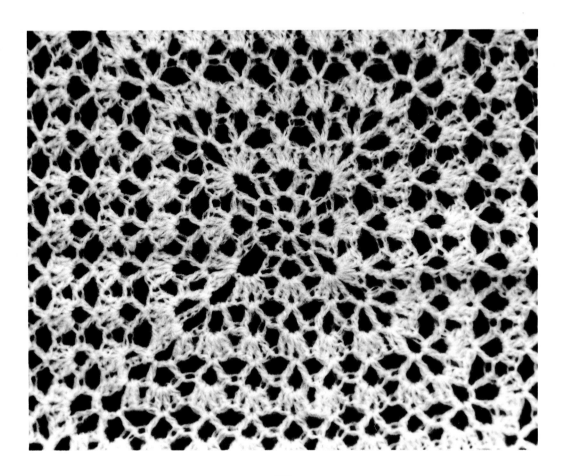

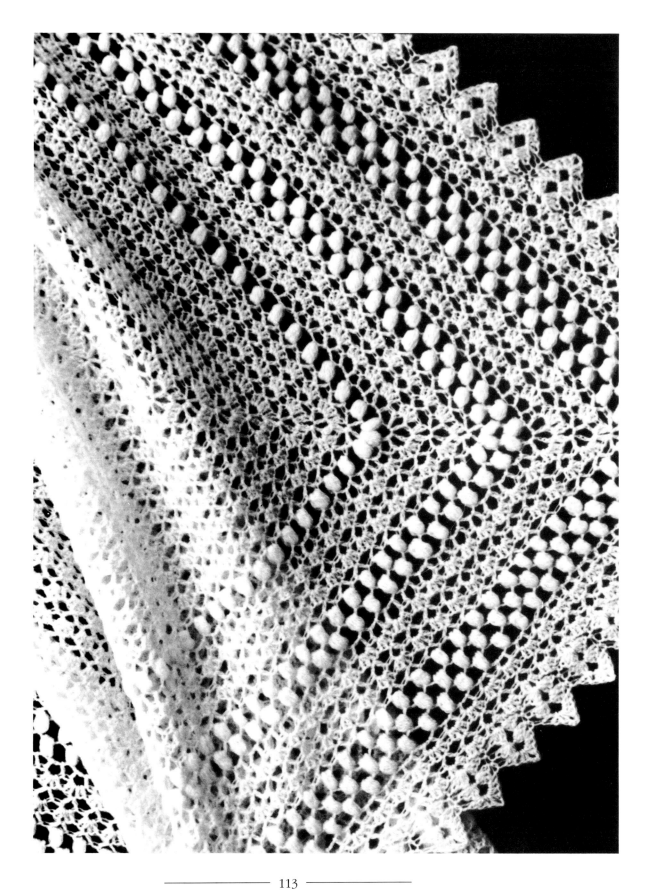

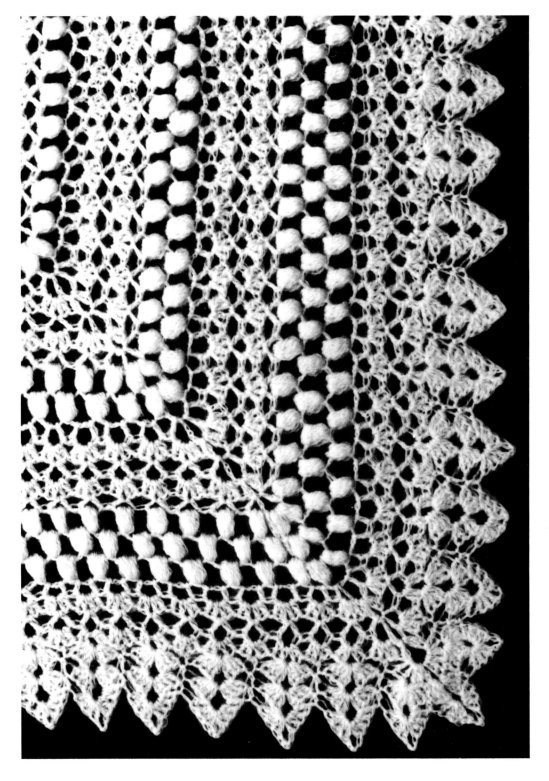

each of next 3 shells, 1tr into corner space, 3ch, ss to 3rd of 6ch.

5th round: ss into corner triangle, 6ch, 2tr into same triangle, *(4tr into next triangle) 5 times, (2tr, 3ch, 2tr) into corner triangle. Repeat from * twice more, (4tr into next triangle) 5 times, 1tr into corner triangle, ss to 3rd of 6ch.

6th round: ss into corner space, 6ch, (1tr, 3ch, 1tr) into same space, *(1tr, 3ch, 1tr) into each of next 5 shells, (1tr, 3ch, 1tr, 3ch, 1tr, 3ch, 1tr) into corner space. Repeat from * twice more, (1tr, 3ch, 1tr) into each of next 5 shells, 1tr into corner space, 3ch, ss to 3rd of 6ch.

Repeat the 5th and 6th rounds, gradually increasing the sides, for the size required, and ending with a 6th round.

Inner border

Directions for working puff stitches are given with *Feather and Puff* stitch (see page 62).

1st round: ss into corner triangle, *3ch, (1 puff, 3ch, 1 puff) into corner triangle, (3ch, 1 puff into next triangle) all along the side. Repeat from * 3 times more, 3ch, ss to top of first puff.

2nd round: ss into centre of corner ch, 6ch, (1tr, 3ch, 1tr) into corner space, *(1tr, 3ch, 1tr) into every space along the side, (1tr, 3ch, 1tr, 3ch, 1tr, 3ch, 1tr) into corner space. Repeat from * twice more, (1tr, 3ch, 1tr) into every space along the side, 1tr into first corner space, 3ch, ss to 3rd of 6ch.

Work 5th and 6th rounds of the ground pattern, twice.

Work 2 rounds of puff stitches followed by the ground pattern as before.

Work 3 rounds of puff stitches followed by the ground pattern as before, but ending with a final round of shells.

Edging

Continue from the diagram, ending each round in the usual way. The base row of the diagram represents the final round of shells on the inner border.

This square design has a *Triangular Ground* pattern, with an inner border of *Diagonal Eye* and an outer edging of *Double Fan and Shell* (see pages 21, 34 and 42 respectively).

The shawl shown was worked in 2-ply Shetland wool using a 4.50mm hook. For a guide to yarn requirements see the section in Preliminary Planning. Set aside one-quarter of the total yarn allowance for the outer edging, and divide the remainder into two, using half for the central ground, and half for the inner border.

Start at the centre with 6ch, ss to join into a ring.

1st round: 5ch, 1tr into ring, (2ch, 1tr into ring) 6 times, 2ch, ss to 3rd of 5ch at beginning.

2nd round: ss into next space, 5ch, (1tr, 1ch, 1tr) into same space, *(1tr, 1ch, 1tr) into next space to make a triangle, (1tr, 1ch, 1tr, 1ch, 1tr, 1ch, 1tr) into following space to make a triple-triangle. Repeat from * twice more, 1 triangle into next space, 1tr into first space, 1ch, ss to 3rd of 5ch.

3rd round: ss into corner triangle, 5ch, 1 triangle into same corner triangle, *(1 triangle into next space between triangles) twice, 1 triple-triangle into corner triangle. Repeat from * twice more, (1 triangle into next space

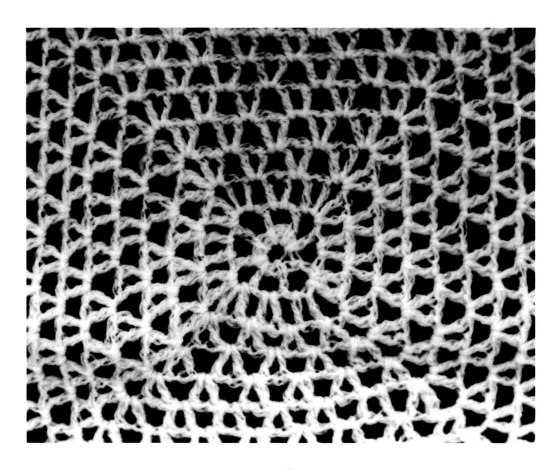

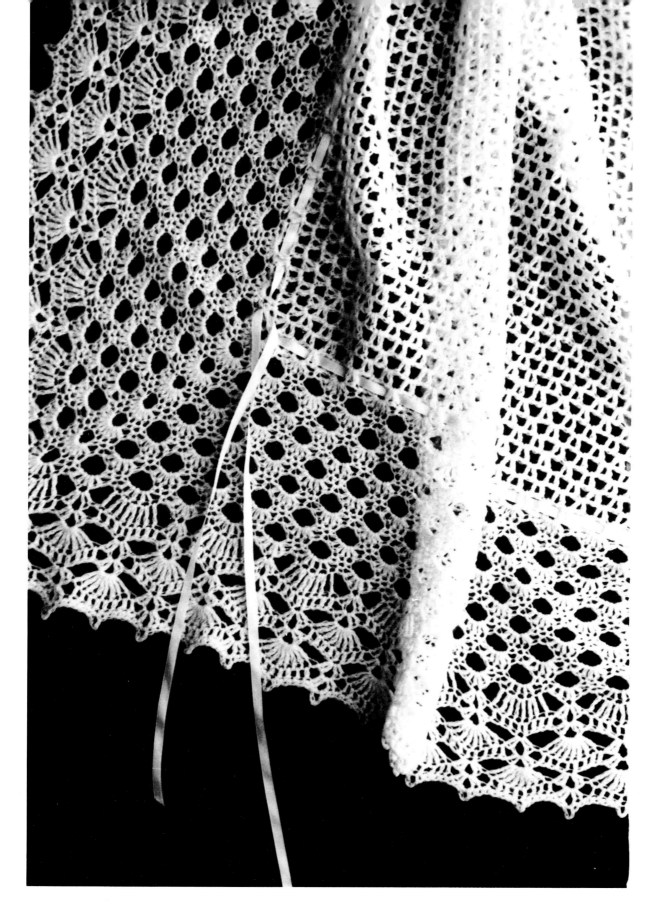

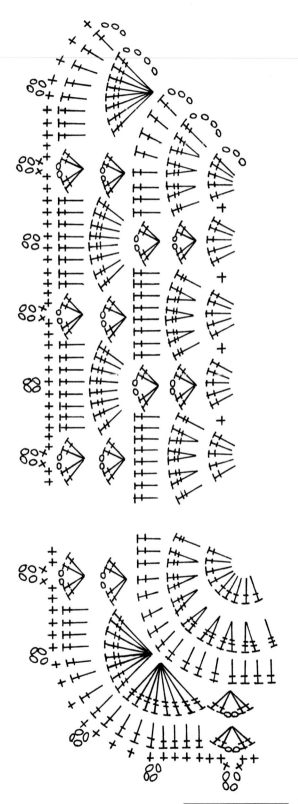

between triangles) twice, 1tr into corner triangle, 1ch, ss to 3rd of 5ch.

4th round: ss into corner triangle, 5ch, 1 triangle into same corner triangle, *(1 triangle into next space between triangles) 3 times, 1 triple-triangle into corner triangle. Repeat from * twice more, (1 triangle into next space between triangles) 3 times, 1tr into corner triangle, 1ch, ss to 3rd of 5ch.

Continue in this way, adding extra triangles on each round, for the size required, and ending with an even number of triangles on each side (not including the triple-triangles).

Inner border

1st round: ss into corner triangle, 3ch, 5tr into same corner triangle, *1dc into next space between triangles, 5tr into following space between triangles. Repeat from * all around, working 9tr into each corner triangle, and ending with 3tr into corner triangle at beginning, ss to top of 3ch.

2nd round: 3ch, miss 1tr, 1dc into each of following 3tr, *3ch, 1dc into 2nd tr of next group, 1dc into each of following 2tr. Repeat from * all around, working (3dc, 3ch, 3dc) into each 9tr corner, and ending the final corner with 3dc.

3rd round: ss into corner loop, 3ch, 5tr into same loop, *1dc into 2nd dc, 5tr into next 3ch loop. Repeat from * all around, working 9tr into each corner loop, and ending the final corner with 3tr into loop, ss to top of 3ch.

Repeat 2nd and 3rd rounds for the size required, ending with a 3rd round and with an odd number of 5tr groups along each side.

Edging

Continue from the diagram, ending each round with ss in the usual way. The base row of the diagram represents the final round of the inner border. Repeat the 3rd and 4th rounds of edging once more, or for the depth required, before working the final outer round.

This square design has *Double Treble Fans* as a centre, with *Alternating Fan and Triangle* as an inner border and *Feather and Bar* as an outer edging (see pages 40, 44 and 60 respectively).

The shawl shown was worked in singles wool, 75 tex, using a 4.00mm hook. For a guide to yarn requirements see the section in Preliminary Planning. Set aside one-quarter of the total yarn allowance for the outer edging. Divide the remainder into two, using half for the centre, and half for the inner border.

Start at the centre with 5ch, ss to join into a ring.

1st round: 4ch, 23dtr into ring, ss to top of 4ch at beginning.

2nd round: 4ch, 4dtr into same place as ss, *miss 2dtr of previous round, 1dc into next dtr, miss 2dtr, 9dtr into following dtr. Repeat from * twice more, miss 2dtr, 1dc into next dtr, 4dtr into same place as 4dtr at beginning, ss to top of 4ch.

3rd round: 4ch, 4dtr into same place as ss, miss 1dtr, 1dc into next dtr, *5dtr into next dc, 1dc into 3rd dtr of next group, 9dtr into 5th dtr, 1dc into 7th dtr. Repeat from * twice more, 5dtr into next dc, 1dc into 3rd dtr of next corner group, 4dtr into same place as 4dtr at beginning, ss to top of 4ch.

4th round: 4ch, 4dtr into same place as ss, miss 1dtr, 1dc into next dtr, *(5dtr into next dc, 1dc into 3rd dtr of next fan) twice, 9dtr into 5th dtr of corner fan, 1dc into 7th dtr. Repeat from * twice more, (5dtr, 1dc) twice as before, 4dtr into same place as 4dtr at beginning, ss to top of 4ch.

Continue in this way, working one extra fan on each side for every round, for the size required.

Inner border

1st round: 6ch, 1dtr into same place as last ss, 2ch, miss 1dtr, 1dc into next dtr, *2ch, (1dtr, 2ch, 1dtr) into next dc to make a triangle, 2ch, 1dc into centre dtr of next fan. Repeat from * all around, but at each corner work 1dc into 3rd dtr, 2ch, 1 triangle into 5th dtr, 1 triangle into 6th dtr, 2ch, 1dc into 8th dtr. End with 1 triangle into 4th dtr at corner, ss to 4th of 6ch.

2nd round: ss into first triangle, 4ch, 4dtr into same triangle, *1dc into next dc, 5dtr into next triangle. Repeat from * all around, working two consecutive 5dtr fans at each corner. End with a final corner fan, ss to top of 4ch.

3rd round: 6ch, 1dtr into same place as ss, *2ch, 1dc into centre dtr of next fan, 2ch, 1 triangle into next dc. Repeat from * all around, working two consecutive triangles at each corner. End with a final corner triangle, ss to 4th of 6ch.

Repeat 2nd and 3rd rounds as required, ending with a 3rd round and an odd number of triangles along each side.

Edging

Continue from the diagram, ending each round with ss in the usual way. The base row of the diagram represents the final round of the inner border.

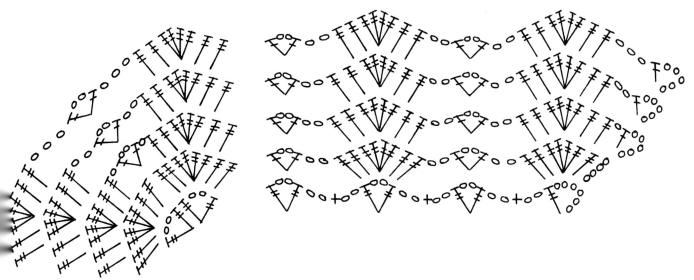

Bibliography

Publications marked * contain historical information.

Dawson, Mary M., *A Complete Guide to Crochet Stitches,* Hodder & Stoughton, 1973

Goldberg, Rhoda Ochser, *The New Crochet Dictionary,* Robert Hale Ltd, 1987

The Harmony Guide to Crochet Stitches, Lyric Books Ltd, 1986

Konior, Mary, *Heritage Crochet – An Analysis,* * Dryad Press Ltd, 1987

Matthews, Anne, *The Vogue Dictionary of Crochet Stitches,* David & Charles, 1987

Stearns, Ann, *The Batsford Book of Crochet,* * B.T. Batsford Ltd, 1981

Turner, Pauline, *Creative Design in Crochet,* B.T. Batsford Ltd, 1983

Turner, Pauline, *Crochet,* * Shire Publications Ltd, 1984

Turner, Pauline, *The Technique of Crochet,* B.T. Batsford Ltd, 1987

Victorian Crochet by Weldon and Company, * Dover Publications Inc., 1974

For information on yarn count systems:

Lorant, Tessa, *The Batsford Book of Hand and Machine Knitting,* B.T. Batsford Ltd, 1980

Lorant, Tessa, *Yarns for the Knitter,* Thorn Press, 1980

Spencer, David, *Knitting Technology,* Pergamon Press, 1983

Manufacturers and Suppliers

Suppliers marked * offer a mail order service, useful for overseas buyers.

UK

Shetland lace wool

Jamieson & Smith*
90 North Road
Lerwick
Shetland Isles ZE1 0PQ

Creativity*
15 Downing Street
Farnham
Surrey GU9 7PB

Creativity
45 New Oxford Street
London WC1

James Templeton & Son Ltd*
Mill Street
Ayr KA7 1TL

Patons 2-ply baby wool

Patons & Baldwins Ltd
P.O. Box, McMullen Road
Darlington
Co. Durham DL1 1YQ

Ries Wools*
243 High Holborn
London WC1V 7DZ

John Lewis
Oxford Street
London W1A 1EX

Creativity
(addresses above)

The Readicut Wool Co Ltd*
Terry Mills
Ossett
West Yorkshire WF5 9SA

2-ply wool on cones

Brockwell Wools*
Stansfield Mill
Triangle
Sowerby Bridge
West Yorkshire HX6 3LZ

T. Forsell & Son Ltd
Blaby Road
South Wigstone
Leicester LE8 2SG

J. & R. Knitting Machines*
13B Bridge Street
Witney
Oxfordshire OX8 6DA

Creativity,
(addresses above)

2-ply acrylic yarn on cones

F.W. Bramwell & Co Ltd*
Unit 5, Metcalf Drive
Altham Lane
Altham
Accrington BB5 5TU

Knitcraft Knitting Machines Ltd*
P.O. Box 121
West Drayton
Middlesex UB7 7JN

Knitmaster
39-45 Cowleaze Road
Kingston upon Thames
Surrey KT2 6DY

J. & R. Knitting Machines
(address above)

Singles wool (one-ply)

Brockwell Wools
(address above)

J. & R. Knitting Machines
(address above)

US, CANADA, AUSTRALIA AND SOUTH AFRICA

Shetland lace wool

Tomato Factory Yarn Co
8 Church Street
Lambertville
New Jersey 08530
USA

Lacis
2982 Adeline Street
Berkeley
California 94703
USA

The Woolgatherer Inc.
1502 Twentyfirst Street, NW
Washington D.C. 20036
USA

Schoolhouse Press
6899 Cary Bluff
Pittsville
Wisconsin 54466
USA

2-ply wool by T. Forsell & Son

Plymouth Yarns
P.O. Box 28
500 Layfayette Street
Bristol
Pennsylvania 19007
USA

Tanunda Wool Craft
1/76 Murray Street
Tanunda
South Australia 5352

Westrade Sales Inc.
2711 No.3 Road
Richmond
BC V6X 2B2
Canada

Bond Africa
P.O. Box 3778
Bloemfontein 9300
South Africa

**2-ply acrylic yarn by
F.W. Bramwell & Co**
Bramwell Yarns
Box 8244
Midland
Texas 79708
USA

Westrade Sales Inc.
(address above)

Tessa B. Knits
98 Norma Road
Myaree
Fremantle
Western Australia 6154

poncho 94
popcorn stitch 62
puff stitches 62–3, 64–5, 101–3, 106–8,
    112–15

R

reversibility 70

S

Shell and Bar Pattern 15, 74, 80, 112, 115
Shell and Feather Shawl 76–7
Shell and Leaf Shawl 74–5
Shell and Net Pattern 26–7, 84
Shell Diamond Shawl 84–7
Shell Pattern, Basic 7, 13
Shells and Triangles Pattern 17, 112–15
Shetland knitting 7, 52
Spider and Block Pattern 30–31, 92
Spreading Fans Pattern 48–9
square shawls 69
    worked in diagonal rows 94–5, 101–3,
        104–5
    worked in rounds 74–5, 76–7, 81–3, 84–7,
        88–9, 92–3, 98–100, 112–15, 116–19,
        120–23
Star Lattice Pattern 23
star stitch 9, 20
stitches, basic 11
symbols 11

T

Tennis Shawl 106–8
tension 11, 71
Three-in-One Shawl 116–19
treble blocks 7, 30, 88–95
Treble Block Shawl 94–5
treble ground 96–7, 98 100, 101–3, 105
treble net 7, 106–7, 109–10
Triangular Ground Pattern 21, 116–18
Triangular Shawl 109–11
triangular shawls 40, 69–70, 90–91, 109–11

W

Waved Panels Pattern 54–5
Waved Treble Shawl 98–100
Waves Pattern 50–51, 98
Willow Pattern Shawl 101–3

Y

yarns 11, 71